MARTIN
LIBRARY

IN MEMORY OF

PROFESSOR WILLIAM PARK
(PSU)

BY
MARY ANNE BACAS

WOODS & PEOPLE

WOODS & PEOPLE

PUTTING FORESTS ON THE MAP

DAVID FOOT

To my young grandsons Jonny and Edward, in the hope that you get as much pleasure living with trees as I have.

First published 2010

The History Press
The Mill, Brimscombe Port
Stroud, Gloucestershire, GL5 2QG
www.thehistorypress.co.uk

British Library Cataloguing in Publication Data.
A catalogue record for this book is available from the British Library.

ISBN 978 0 7524 5278 4

Typesetting and origination by The History Press
Printed in Great Britain
Manufacturing managed by Jellyfish Print Solutions Ltd

CONTENTS

ACKNOWLEDGEMENTS

When I set out to write this book, I did not know what I was letting myself in for; both as regards the time it would take and the road that it would lead me down. It evolved, as will be obvious, from a mixture of library research, personal knowledge and impressions acquired over many years of involvement with trees. So it would be wrong to start these acknowledgements without an expression of gratitude to all the people, in several organisations, who, over the years, have helped to shape my experiences and thinking. That said, it is inevitable that some of my past colleagues and present friends will not agree with the particular emphasis I have given to events or necessarily share the words and sentiments with which I describe them.

Graham Hamilton, Michael Medcalf and Jenny Claridge read the book in its entirety at different stages in its preparation and offered many suggestions. I am very grateful to Graham, Mike and Jenny for the time and effort they put into what at times must have seemed an uphill task! Of course, the responsibility for any mistakes is entirely mine.

Several other people helped me with advice, assistance or offers of help along the way. They include Bridget Bloom, Steve and Nadine Cooper, Elaine Dick, Julian Evans, Peter Freer-Smith, Tim Rollinson, Marcus Sangster and my son Mark Foot. I am most grateful to all of them for their help.

The library and photographic staff of the Forestry Commission have been generous with their time, particularly Catherine Oldham, Eleanor Harland, George Gate, Isobel Cameron and Neill Campbell – thank you all.

Most of all I want to thank my wife, Nina, who encouraged me to start the book and was always confident that it would progress from an idea to a finished draft that would 'see the light of day'. She will now get that long-awaited holiday!

Picture Acknowledgements

I am grateful to the Forestry Commission for providing pictures 10, 12, 15–17, 21–2, 24–6, 29, 31–41, and to the Royal Forestry Society for permission to use picture 6. Other pictures have been supplied by the National Museums of Scotland (1, 2), Getty Images (3, 7–9, 11, 14, 18, 27–8), the High Wycombe Library, Buckinghamshire (4), the Bucks Free Press (13, 30), the Falkirk Museums (19) and the Press Association (20).

Figure 1 is reproduced by permission of the Forestry Commission and the Ordnance Survey.

NOTE ON AREA
EXPRESSIONS

Until the 1970s, the common unit for expressing and measuring area was the acre. Then, as part of Britain's policy of metrication, it became common to express areas in hectares. One hectare is the same as 2.47 acres. Despite metrication, the expression of area in terms of acres is still in everyday use. Because most readers will be familiar with both units, area conversions have not been shown in the text. Thus historical references to areas before 1970 are in acres and references thereafter are expressed in hectares.

INTRODUCTION

To a rambler a forest is merely a delightful place to walk in; delightful because of its wild life and colour, its sounds and smells, and in the way it reveals its character little by little. But the woodman sees more in it than this. The forest is to him what the cornfield is to the farmer – a source of profit and the means of livelihood. There is, then, a great difference between exploring a wood for pleasure and regarding it through the eyes of a woodman.[1]

This quotation, from a children's book entitled *The Seasons & the Woodman*, played a big part in getting me into forestry. Written by D.H. Chapman, it had an introduction by the well-known ecologist Frank Fraser Darling and illustrations by C.F. Tunnicliffe. As a boy I had always enjoyed woods as a place to run and play, but never thought of them from the viewpoint of the woodsman or forester. Woods and forests, it is sometimes said, are unique in being where industry and the environment meet, but these two sides of the same coin tend to be separated in people's minds. When I set out to write this story, I wanted to join them together.

We are now at an unusually interesting point in forest history. Hardly a week goes by without some reference in the national newspapers to tree planting. The *Sunday Times* is helping the Woodland Trust to plant its Heartwood Forest to 'exploit the calming effects of woodland therapy'.[2] The *News of the World* wants to help fight climate change by planting a million trees in the 'biggest, most ambitious green project ever undertaken by a national newspaper'.[3] And the Green Alliance, in their *Green Manifesto on Climate Change and the Natural Environment* (September 2009) called for 'significant progress' by 2020 towards a doubling of woodland cover in Britain.[4]

Ninety years ago, it was a very different tree-planting aim that occupied people's minds. Blockades by enemy submarines in the First World War had exposed a critical weakness in Britain's defences. By putting a squeeze on imports of foreign timber, enemy action starved the mining industry of the pit props it needed for coal production. This in turn threatened to halt the manufacture of the steel that was needed for shipbuilding and armaments. Home timber production suddenly became a matter of keen interest to politicians. David Lloyd George in his memoirs described timber as:

> a very badly neglected asset ... There was no more useful contribution to our mortal struggle with the submarine than [the] organisation of our home supplies of timber ... It stripped this island of some of our best forest. Not only most of our hill sides, but large areas once clad in fine timber are now bare and broken.[5]

Even as the war progressed, Lloyd George and his coalition government ordered a review of Britain's forest resources and the drawing-up of a plan to plant trees.

There is a powerful link between these two contrasting themes – the notion of forests as timber reserves illustrated by the wartime thinking of Lloyd George and the present-day approach to tree planting exemplified by the newspaper campaigns of the kind described above. Both themes have the common purpose of reforestation. Britain can claim no moral high ground when it comes to *deforestation*, having largely destroyed its own natural tree cover in prehistoric times. However, it can claim to have a lot of experience of *reforestation*. Because we cleared our forests at an early date, we were the first to think about replanting them. Stimulated initially by the First World War, and later by changing social and economic influences, an extraordinary 7 per cent of the land surface (1.6 million hectares of forest) was added to Britain's tree resource between 1900 and 2010, so increasing the country's forest cover from 5 per cent at the end of the nineteenth century to some 12 per cent today; still, it must be said, almost the lowest percentage in Europe, but increasing all the time.

This book, then, is a popular account of twentieth-century forest and woodland restoration. How have the actions of individuals, government, private landowners and, in more recent times, the voluntary conservation movement shaped the nature of the landscape and of the forests and woods that embellish it? The book makes no claim to be an ecological study, nor is it a technical account of forestry, nor indeed does it make more than a passing mention of ancient forests like the New Forest which are well catered for in more specialist books. Inevitably, it must be selective and personal; all history, they say, reflects the writer's preoccupations and those of the era in which he or she is writing. And since it is impossible to understand the countryside without examining the human factors that have shaped its development, I have tried to place the story in the context of the social and economic circumstances of a quite remarkably transformed century.

I gave some consideration to whether the book should have an all-Britain approach and concluded that this was the right one. The shared threads of economic and social change across England, Scotland and Wales, and the common political background of forest law and policy throughout nearly the whole of the twentieth century (political devolution of forest and countryside matters having taken place in 1998), was reflected in the development of country-wide institutions. The Forestry Commission, for instance, formed in 1919, exercised a common policy on forestry on behalf of successive governments, and the larger representative bodies and voluntary organisations that influenced forest policy were also mainly nationwide.

Turning now to the layout of the book, the first chapter is scene-setting to get to a point where the reader has some feel for the background to the tree-planting history of the twentieth century. Subsequent chapters explore the story in a mainly chronological order, diverting here and there to look at topics of special interest. By the mid-1980s a remarkable change was in the air. In a decade marked by new ideas, agricultural reform and important legislative change, the 'timber-first' philosophy that had prevailed since 1919 gave way to a multi-benefit approach that is still evolving today. The talk now is about the 'non-timber' benefits of trees – trees for wildlife and woods for recreation; trees for shelter on farms; community woods of different kinds; trees for restoring the health of degraded landscapes; and trees as producers of oxygen and storers of carbon. These 'new directions' are the subject of my final chapter.

The rediscovery of these wider functions of trees, woods and forests could not be more timely. Alarmist forecasts about the effect of climate change on Britain's tree landscape continue to worry us. What is certain is that we shall need to plant more trees to maintain the ecological health and diversity of the countryside in testing times. The questions for the future will be how and where, and what approach will truly maximise the benefits of Britain's trees and woods for society. The lessons and experience of forest restoration gained over nearly a hundred years of changing times is what this book is about.

1

BEGINNINGS

For a man keen on hunting, it might have been expected that William the Conqueror would have gathered more information on woods and forests. But woods are not a great source of money, nor have they ever been, and the Domesday Book of 1086 was intended for business purposes rather than pleasure; in other words, for collecting taxes. Domesday helps historians to build up a picture of the social order, how the land was used and, by implication, the extent of woodland decline from prehistoric times. Woodland information in Domesday is scanty and difficult to interpret, but historians have concluded that around 15 per cent of the land surface of Norman England was covered in trees,[1] and probably rather more in Scotland and Wales. The woods that did exist were already much modified by man from the natural tree cover that had once covered Britain like a great cloak after the last Ice Age.

Domesday then, the first detailed description of the more populous parts of Britain, is a good starting point for the book. Norman England, often pictured in the mind's eye as a land of great forests, was in fact a mainly agricultural and pastoral country. And the royal forests, we are told, were not the predominantly tree-covered lands that we usually associate with the word 'forest' today, but a mosaic of woodland, pasture, wetlands, heath and scrub, and scattered settlements and cultivation. More generally, beyond the boundaries of the royal forests, the growing peasant population of medieval times filled out the farming map, making inroads into the areas of 'waste', a process checked at times by periods of economic stagnation or decline when semi-natural woodland re-colonised the medieval fields.

It was still early days in the era of Britain's naval supremacy when we start to hear about timber shortages. Laws to preserve timber for shipbuilding were a regular theme of the sixteenth- and seventeenth-century Acts of Parliament. In 1558, Queen Elizabeth I banned the use of *timber* trees of oak, beech and ash for the making of charcoal within 14 miles of the sea and certain navigable rivers in the south of England and Wales. Oak, of course, above all other tree species, played the key role in shipbuilding, and its availability in large quantities in a range of curved and straight pieces was crucial to the architecture of a 'ship of the line'.

By the sixteenth century, the grip of the old forest laws was fading and the royal forests were breaking up through encroachment and because successive monarchs sold or gave away timber for favours. Meanwhile, the process of estate-building was getting under way. In the late sixteenth and seventeenth century, books and pamphlets on better farming methods started to appear, opening up the fashion for 'improvement' and hastening the process of field enclosure. Enclosure meant better farming, arable as well as pasture, not least because it extinguished the rights of commoners and gave the landlords freedom to manage the land as they wished. Landowners began to drain wet fields and bogs, and clear away inconveniently sited woodland. A remark in a manorial survey of a Shropshire village in 1563 that 'the many enclosures ... are like to destroy the woods' is quoted by the historian D.C. Coleman.[2] He supposes that this comment would have been echoed all over the country. It was probably a reference both to the displacement of managed medieval coppices and the enclosure and 'breaking-in' of 'waste' – extensive areas of common ground that supported the rough open pasture woodlands where villagers grazed their animals and collected firewood.

Planting and Propagation

Exactly when early man in Britain started to plant and cultivate trees, nobody really knows. Dendrologist John White tells us that Bronze Age farmers brought in bundles of English elm plants or cuttings from southeast Europe between 3,000 and 5,000 years ago.[3] Obviously it was the special uses of foreign trees that motivated their introduction; in this case for cattle fodder and bedding. So it was with the Romans. What was more natural than introducing trees from warmer climes as a civilising influence to a conquered land, so adding a touch of familiarity to their surroundings and to their diet – they are thought, for instance, to have introduced several fruit trees and to have planted the sweet chestnut and walnut for their nuts.

Popular history has it that one of the first *woods* to be successfully planted was in Cranbourne Walk within Windsor Great Park in 1580, when an area of 13 acres was sown with acorns by order of Lord Burleigh. We know that his lordship's oak wood survived the browsing attentions of the cattle and deer because, in 1625, it was described as 'a wood of some thousands of tall young oaks, bearing acorns, and giving shelter to cattle, and likely to prove as good timber as any in the kingdom'.

John Evelyn's celebrated tree book *Sylva*, first published in 1664, was the first serious tree reference book and an arboricultural tour de force that is still a pleasure to read today. Although best known for his descriptive diaries of the restoration era, Evelyn was a man of many parts: a courtier to Charles II, a landowner and a passionate lover of trees and gardens. Prompted by the 'waste and destruction' of forests in the Civil War, his book was based on a lecture he had presented to the members of the newly founded Royal Society. The topic, suggested to him by the navy commissioners, was forest decline and the perilous shortage of oak trees for shipbuilding. He could hardly have imagined how durable the message would be in the face of the centuries of further forest decline that followed the publication of his book. Delivered in the typically flowery language of the times, it was a clarion call for more planting: 'Truly the waste and destruction of our woods has been so universal, that I conceive nothing less than a universal plantation of all sorts of trees will supply, and will encounter the defect.'

It might seem that the target of Evelyn's appeal would have been the *royal forests*; falling as they did under crown control, they provided the authorities with a direct and immediate means of remedying the anticipated shortage of timber. But there were two reasons why this did not happen. First, by the end of the Civil War the royal forests were just a shadow of their heyday in Norman times, many of them having passed by grant or sale into private hands. Secondly, they were not the exclusive property of the crown to do with as it wished; rather they included the property and interests of many people with leases or ancient rights. Commoners' ancient rights – as, for example, the grazing of livestock or the right to take wood for fuel – were jealously guarded and could only be set aside by agreement, perhaps with the payment of compensation or through an Act of Parliament.

Something of the problem can be gleaned from the enquiries of a government commission set up at the end of the eighteenth century to report on the 'state and condition of the woods, forests and land revenue of the crown'. In the commission's seventh report, published in 1793,[4] the many interests in the crown woods were described as a 'confused mixture of rights', such that the crown's attempt to manage the forest was a 'perpetual struggle of jarring interests in which no party can improve his own share without hurting that of another'. This then was no simple background for an imposed programme of tree planting, even before the days of planners or planning! A number of Acts for the 'increase and preservation of timber' had been passed in the later years of the seventeenth century and into the eighteenth. The most important ones permitted enclosure and tree planting in the two great surviving royal forests – the New Forest in Hampshire and the Forest of Dean in Gloucestershire. But what was successfully established with trees was, it seems, limited and can almost be dismissed from the reckoning in the big picture of post-Evelyn planting. The same 1793 report recorded that the crown forests 'in his Majesty's reign' (George III, 1760–1820) had provided 'not more than one twelfth part' of the oak required by the navy shipyards.

The prospects for tree planting on private estates at the end of the Civil War were a lot more encouraging than those that existed in the crown woods. Confiscated estates had been returned to their owners while, more generally, landowners were feeling confident about the prospects for a settled future. Land in the late seventeenth century became one of the safest investments, and the estate owners put in hand improvements and enlargements. Evelyn recommended that landowners 'at their first coming to their Estates, and as soon as they get children, should seriously think of this [tree] propagation also'. His ideas, it seems, fell on receptive soil. Evelyn's book was a great success and, not a man to hide his achievements, he boasted in the 1706 edition (addressed by Evelyn in 1678 to King Charles II) that 'many millions of timber-trees have been propagated and planted ... at the institution, and by the sole direction of this work'.

Although Evelyn's headline appeal was the planting of oak trees for the navy, he nonetheless cast far and wide for his 'universal plantation of all sorts of trees'. His contents list for *Sylva* included fruit trees and ornamentals, and his tree descriptions were enlivened with stories and gossip from his self-imposed exile in Europe during the Civil War. Europe, in a way, became the inspiration for the tree craze that followed the Civil War. The Grand Tour introduced wealthy young men to art and architecture, capturing their interest in the aesthetics of landscape and introducing them to the visual appeal of new kinds of trees. In the late seventeenth and eighteenth centuries, landowners returned to Britain from their European travels with a determination to improve the look of their own family acres, planting pines, larches, birches, elms, beeches, sycamore, limes and chestnuts in their tens of thousands.

Lancelot 'Capability' Brown was another historical figure with a special enthusiasm for trees. Where Evelyn was an academic, Brown was a practical man whose legacy was his physical achievements on the ground rather than his written words. Brown came to the fore as a garden contractor to the great and the good in the second half of the eighteenth century, and is famed for the natural look of his landscaping designs. Christopher Hussey, the pioneering architectural historian, once described Brown as the 'Director-General' of trees.[5] This was not because Brown planted trees in great numbers (though he did), but because of his ability to see beyond the immediate view and to picture how they would look after his lifetime. 'While [he] could not hope to see the finished picture', Hussey says, Brown was 'animated by the faith and foresight to visualise that which we now too readily accept as the gift of Providence or Nature'.

Brown's designs, and those of his self-appointed successor Humphrey Repton, were a showpiece for the landscaping effects of trees. Trees added stature, maturity and an aura of naturalness to the engineered setting of the great houses they worked on. Trees channelled the eye, opened up vistas, masked what they thought of as untidiness and brought shelter and privacy from the agricultural hinterland beyond. Brown's typical parkland was designed with an encircling band of trees, broken by occasional openings to give just glimpses of the local landmarks; Repton ventured that 'a ploughed field was no fit sight from a gentleman's elegant mansion'.

Beyond the boundaries of the great houses, the enclosure movement was approaching its climax in the latter part of Brown's professional career. The parliamentary enclosures in central England were at their height between 1760 and 1820. How did woods and woodland fare in this great reorganisation of the land? While the general trend of tree decline continued, it seems that there were now some gains to set against the losses. New woods were fitted into the developing mosaic of fields and hedgerows where the soils or the lie of the land was unsuitable for agriculture. In the lowlands, many new coppice woods were created by sowing seed or planting cuttings, so replacing some of the medieval coppices that had fallen victim to the changes. During the Napoleonic War (1773–1815), buoyant wood prices reinforced the fashion for tree planting. The very process of enclosure stimulated a surge of demand for wooden artefacts of all kinds – fencing materials, tools, barns, bridges, carts and so on. The idea of managing woods as 'high forest' rather than by coppicing was catching on. Conifers were planted on former areas of waste and on previously unenclosed hill ground in the upland regions. In the previously marginalised crown forests, a renewed planting effort was made. Starting in 1808, around 33,000 acres were planted in the New Forest and Forest of Dean.

The Commercial Spirit Catches On

an oak must grow an hundred years, or more, until it comes to maturity; but profits arising from tillage or pasture are more certain and immediate, and perhaps as great: It cannot, therefore, be expected that many private individuals will lay out money on the expectation of advantages which they themselves can have no chance to enjoy: Commerce and industry seek for, and are supported by, speedy returns of gain, however small; and the more generally the commercial spirit shall prevail in this country, the less probability is there that planting of woods, for the advantages of prosperity, will be preferred to the immediate profits of agriculture. It is accordingly in the northern, or mountainous parts of the kingdom chiefly, and on land unfit for tillage, where any great plantations have lately been made; and these are mostly of fir.

For all its commercial insights, this quotation from the 1793 commission report does not completely explain why trees in Britain were pushed so completely to the margins of agriculture in the course of the enclosure movement. The industrial revolution was under way and timber consumption by industry, together with a rising population, should surely have suggested a terrible shortage.

There is a simple explanation for the complacency and disinterest. From medieval times, trade was preferred to forestry, and Britain came to rely on the closed world of the timber importer. Oak timber, for instance, which was still common enough in medieval times, was nevertheless imported from the virgin forests of Poland and the Baltic countries from the thirteenth century[6] because the long straight lengths needed for the construction of large and important buildings were already scarce in the more accessible parts of the British Isles. Oak timbers could be obtained more cheaply from abroad than from the inland parts of Britain. Ships' masts of pine or fir were imported from the Americas and Baltic countries, and, by the eighteenth century, mahogany for furniture-making had become fashionable, brought in from the West Indies and South America. By then, what had started as the import of small amounts of timber for specific markets had developed into a flood of every kind of timber. With the growth of its empire and of the Royal Navy to protect its merchant ships, Britain became the biggest importer of timber and wood products in the world. Why then grow timber at home or preserve forest when it could so readily and cheaply be bought abroad?

The *commercial* appeal of imported timbers played a critical part in this trend. Very few of the tree species in Britain's natural forest are of commercial importance in the timber and wood product markets of Britain today, and the usefulness and adaptability of imported timber was already a major influence in the eighteenth century. Imported softwood became the preferred wood for building and everyday carpentry. Compared to oak as a building material, softwood was easier and quicker to cut, lighter to carry about and easier to fix in building structures, and above all much cheaper to buy. Among the conifers, only Scots pine among Britain's native trees is of commercial importance, but this too is seen as an imported timber (redwood) outside its natural range in the Highlands of Scotland.

As such, home-grown timber played second fiddle to imported timber from an early age, although there seems to have been no doubt that some of the introduced conifers would produce useful timber when they were grown in Britain. Norway spruce, for instance – the typical 'whitewood' or White Deal of the timber merchant – was introduced in the sixteenth century. Traveller, writer and diarist Daniel Defoe in his 'Tour' of Scotland (1729) seems to have been confident of its usefulness, remarking with optimism: 'In a few years, Scotland will not need to send to Norway for Timber or Deal, but will have sufficient of her own and perhaps be able to furnish England too with considerable Quantities.'[7] Another great traveller, the agricultural diarist Arthur Young, when on a tour of the Vale of Tywi in the 1770s, wrote in his journal that locally grown 'spruce fir' was 'very good; almost as white as Norway deals'.[8]

European larch was another interesting tree to eighteenth- and nineteenth-century landowners because it was seen as a substitute for oak in shipbuilding. Not only did it grow more quickly – 75 years rather than 150 years or more for oak – but it grew well in the more testing conditions of soil and climate that were typical of the upland estates in Scotland and Wales. The Reverend C.A. Johns, a late nineteenth-century writer on trees, thought larch to be:

better adapted for naval architecture than any other timber. It becomes harder
and more durable by age in a ship. It holds iron as firmly as Oak, but, unlike
Oak, it does not corrode iron. It does not shrink; it possesses the valuable
property of resisting damp. It catches fire with difficulty, and it does not splin-
ter when struck by a canon-ball.[9]

Famously, the Dukes of Atholl were the first landowners to establish
European larch on a big scale, clothing the then barren valley of the River
Tay between Dunkeld and Blair Atholl in a way that, even today, grabs the
attention of travellers on the A9 for its particular charm. The dukes planted
over 21 million trees between 1730 and 1830 on some 15,000 acres of
ground. The legendary fourth duke – the so-called 'Planting Duke' – was
the greatest advocate of the species: 'There is no name that stands so high,
and so deservedly high, in the list of successful planters, as that of the late
John, Duke of Athole', says Johns. 'His Grace planted, in the last years of his
life, 6,500 Scotch acres of mountain ground solely with larch which, in the
course of seventy-two years from the time of planting, will be a forest of
timber fit for the building of the largest class of ships in His Majesty's navy.'

Less commonly known is that European larch also made an appearance
in the upland landscapes of eighteenth-century Wales. Elisabeth Inglis-
Jones, in her book *Peacocks in Paradise*, tells how one Cardiganshire (now
Ceredigion) landowner, the eccentric Thomas Johnes, was determined to
transform the denuded and inhospitable hills of his Hafod Estate to a 'green
cloak of woodland' where 'nothing would be allowed to offend the naked
eye'. We might surmise that Johnes got his inspiration from the Atholl dukes
when he attended Edinburgh University in the 1760s, before leaving for
the 'well-beaten' track across Europe. When he inherited Hafod in 1769,
he set his mind on the complete rehabilitation of the estate, both farming
and forestry, and between 1795 and 1801 planted 2,065,000 trees, half of
them larch, which 'flourished vigorously in exposed places' and, for the rest,
'every variety of timber tree was represented in his woods and all seemed to
thrive'. His tree-planting successes won him several gold medals from the
London (later Royal) Society of Arts. Trees, it was said, 'prospered for him as
nothing else did'. Unfortunately, they and his agricultural improvements led
him into debt and poor health, and ultimately to the sale of Hafod. Despite
his disappointments, he 'talked of Hafod as a paradise, and of his improvements with rapture, as if he had never met with a single disappointment in
his life'.[10]

These great planting projects were not just the work of a small eccentric band of tree enthusiasts. The list of the great and good who took an interest in trees was formidable. 'Nicol's Planter's Kalendar', prepared in 1812 by nurseryman E. Sang of Kirkcaldy in Fife (whose plant lists went to land-owners all over the country), contained the following:

> at no period of the history of this country has a spirit for planting more pre-vailed among private individuals, than within these last sixty years; whether we consider the decrease of trees in our natural forests, the high price of timber, or the difficulty in obtaining foreign supplies of that article. The extensive scale on which plantations ... particularly in Scotland, have lately been conducted, certainly reflects very high honour on the landholders. The business of planting is now established on a broad basis, and has become more or less the case of every great landowner in the Kingdom.[11]

Nineteenth-century Introductions

There was an important phase of tree introductions still to come when 'Nicol's Planter's Kalender' was published. During the nineteenth century, the existing trickle of new tree introductions turned into a flood, with plant collectors scouring the globe to find new and interesting species under the patronage of wealthy landowners and with the sponsorship of botanical bodies such as Kew (founded in 1759) and the Royal Horticultural Society (in 1804).

David Douglas' nineteenth-century journey into the interior of British Columbia stands out for its benefits to forestry as well as adding now famil-iar plants to almost every present-day garden in Britain. As the son of a stonemason from Scone in Perthshire, Douglas came from humble and unlikely beginnings, becoming an apprentice gardener at Scone Palace at the age of only 11. There he developed a lively and intelligent interest in plants, progressing through a number of appointments to work at the botanic gardens in Glasgow, and eventually stepping up to become a plant collector for the Royal Horticultural Society.

Douglas' journal captures his great delight at what he saw on a bright but misty April morning in 1825, when the three-mast sailing ship, the *William and Anne*, entered the mouth of the Columbia River on the Pacific coast of North America, still then one of the great unexplored areas of the world. He describes how he saw through the lingering mist the great Douglas firs (the tree that was named after him) that were 'thickly clad to the very ground with widespreading pendent branches, and from the gigantic size they attain … form one of the most striking and truly graceful objects in nature'.[12]

The significance of the coastal fringe of north-west America to botanists and foresters is its climate. The oceanic climate of that coastline between Vancouver Island and the Queen Charlotte Islands – the so-called coastal 'fog belt' – closely matches that of western Britain, with its moist, mild and variable weather, so providing the right conditions for many of its native plants to flower and flourish in Britain. Douglas' expedition added over 200 new species to the botanical map of the world. His tree introductions, as well as the Douglas fir, included the Sitka spruce, the Grand and Noble firs, and – from a later expedition – the ubiquitous Radiata pine (Monterey pine), now widely planted as a commercial species in the southern hemisphere (see for instance Chapter 7). Douglas knew them all as 'pines' and when writing to his sponsor in Britain said: 'you will begin to think that I manufacture pines at my pleasure.'[13]

Probably the most controversial of Douglas' many tree introductions was the Sitka spruce, now Britain's most important commercial tree and ironically, in modern times, a totem for the conservation movement in north-west America. Sitka in Britain came to epitomise the conflict between environmentalists and foresters; we return to this in Chapter 5. One side resented the planting of Sitka in the cherished open landscapes of upland Britain, while the other side saw merit and opportunity in its commercial qualities – vigorous growth on poor soils and a high degree of climatic hardiness. Foresters argued that it filled an obvious gap in Britain's natural flora, there being no native timber tree so well suited to the prevailing cool, wet and windy climate of western Britain. Douglas himself seems to have contemplated benefit in every direction: in the Sitka's appearance as well as its growth, noting in his journal that it:

> possesses one great advantage by growing to a very large size on the northern declivities of the mountain in poor thin damp soils … it would thrive in such places in Britain where even Scots pine finds no shelter … This if introduced would profitably clothe the bleak barren hilly parts of Scotland … besides improving the beauty of the country.[14]

Douglas' precious collections of tree seeds were quickly snapped up by nurserymen and the fashion-conscious Victorian landowners keen to try out the latest tree introductions. Seed and plants were scarce and costly, so most of his collections were planted out as single specimens or small groups in arboreta or in the grounds of the big houses; a few even survive today. Strangely, after Douglas' insightful comments, Sitka's timber-producing qualities were hardly noticed for nearly 90 years after its introduction, until it was 'rediscovered' as a forest tree in the first quarter of the twentieth century.

Decline in the Rural Economy

By the 1820s, the enclosure movement had slowed and most of the great areas of waste that had existed a hundred years earlier had been brought into cultivation or, in much more modest amounts, planted with trees. In the lowlands, the estate-improvement period was coming to an end and, with it, the creation of new woods. Interest in the land and the availability of money to invest in it had declined in the face of social and economic change. In the uplands, however, where there was still plenty of suitable land available, tree planting continued, particularly in Scotland.

According to the economist E.J.T. Collins, the forest area of upland Scotland doubled between 1845 and 1924.[15] Tree planting in the uplands was often carried out to improve sheep walks and provide shelter for cattle (See Picture 22). Many Scottish landowners, keen to improve their recently acquired shooting estates, experimented with conifer introductions. The famous Redwood avenue at Benmore near Dunoon in Argyllshire (later owned by the Younger family of brewing fame, see Chapter 2) was planted in 1863 and 'wide tracts' of the estate were also planted between 1871 and 1883. Between 1873 and 1910, Sir John Ramsden planted 10,400 acres at Ardverikie in Inverness-shire, best known today as the setting of the BBC's *Monarch of the Glen* series. More generally, the great emerging industries of coal, steel and the railways lured people away from the land because they paid higher wages, leaving workers in rural areas at the bottom of the pay league. A population census in 1851 revealed that the urban population of Britain was, for the first time, greater than the rural, and with it wealth and influence migrated to the towns and the new industrial heartlands. Significantly, for the politicians, rural votes were no longer the main priority.

Victorian agriculture was a story of contrasting fortunes. From a state of depression after the Napoleonic Wars, farming conditions had improved by the beginning of Queen Victoria's reign in 1837, and the years between 1850 and the mid-1870s are often described as its golden age. The reason for this was a surge in growth of demand for farm products. The development of transport opened up the town and city markets to fresh food. Canals and much-improved road systems were followed in the 1830s and '40s by the railways, much to the advantage of farmers. They could now transport and sell their fresh produce in the market towns and, by the same token, return home with the latest ideas in agricultural husbandry, and with new tools and machinery for cultivating the land.

However, it is the ill-fortune of the landowners and their declining investment in the land that is the main story here. The tide turned in the 1870s when farming, and the great estates with it, went into an economic slide that lasted until the Second World War. The seeds of the depression had been sown by the repeal of the Corn Laws in 1846 and the move to free trade more generally thereafter. With farmers no longer protected from foreign imports of grain, and a run of bad harvests in the 1870s, the door was open to food imports from the emerging New World. For farmers and landowners, retrenchment was the only solution; large areas of cereal crops were given up or converted to pasture and job losses on the farms hastened to a new level. A.D. Hall (later Sir Daniel Hall), one of the great names in British agriculture and a one-time President Secretary to the Board of Agriculture and Fisheries, summed up the attitude of the landowners in the 1890s in these words:

> In the main landowners had accepted the position that there was little future in farming, that the development of their estates did not offer an outlet for their energies or capital comparable to those available elsewhere, and that their function was to be easy with their tenants in return for the sport and social status that the ownership of land conferred.[16]

Against this background of agricultural decline, woodland management also suffered from the economic and social changes of the times brought on by technical advance and the pressures of the free market. There were no sudden disasters – none of the catastrophic harvests that had happened in agriculture – just a steady decline in the traditional markets and a waning of landowners' interest in their woods.

Declining Wood Markets

In the second half of the nineteenth century, we catch only the dying embers of perhaps the most important historical wood industry of all. The production of charcoal for iron-smelting had been an industry of supreme significance to the industrialisation of Britain, occupying at one time many tens of thousands of people in woods around the country. The ancient connection between woods and iron working was broken when Abraham Darby, in 1709, discovered a method of smelting iron ore with coke. The iron industry's migration from the forests to the coalfields was a slow one, driven as much by wood availability as it was by the new methods of iron production. In the eighteenth century, wood became scarce and expensive in the iron industry's two greatest traditional areas – the Weald of Sussex and Kent and the Forest of Dean. Yet where wood was cheap and plentiful, new sites were opened up, as for instance around Workington and Furness in north-west England, and in Shropshire, Herefordshire, North and South Wales, and in Scotland. The iron ore, if it could not be found locally, was brought in overland to the forests or by sea. One of the last sites to close was the Lorne furnace on Loch Etive in Argyllshire, which had opened for business around 1753 and shut down in 1876. By then, the transition from charcoal to coke and coal was complete.

Did the charcoaling industry contribute to forest decline? Some historians talk of the ironmasters' cut-and-run activities exploiting the woods and leaving behind only 'sterile, heath-like areas and scrub', while others suppose that the ironmasters managed the woods renewably by coppicing. It was, after all, in their interests to do so. No doubt the truth was a mixture of both.

Tanbark was another great woodland industry which, like charcoal-burning, supported large numbers of people. In many ways it was complimentary to the other wood-using activities because it employed what would have been a waste product, the tree bark. Every market town had at least one tannery where skins and hides were prepared for the leather and shoe industries. In contrast to the dirty and unpopular mainly year-round job of the charcoal burners, the bark harvest was seasonal. Bark-stripping was carried out when the sap was rising between April and June, and at this time of year it took precedence over many other jobs in the estate calendar (see Picture 12). Gangs of workers were assembled for the purpose and whole families were drafted in as casual workers for the peak season. At the height of demand, tanbark was more valuable to landowners than the timber itself, finding a market not just in the local tanneries, but also in a significant export trade. Chepstow, for instance, is cited by William Linnard[17] as one of the main export centres in late eighteenth-century Wales. Drawing for its supplies on the extensive oak woods of the Wye Valley, over 4,000 tons a year were sold there to local tanneries or exported to markets in England and Ireland.

Oak was the favoured tree species and therefore worth the most, though other kinds of tree bark was also used, including birch and larch. Part of the harvest came from managed coppices and part was salvaged from forest trees and trees in parks and hedgerows, the felling of which was timed to take place at the right time of year. Timing was everything; if the bark was not stripped within twenty-four hours of felling, it would be doubly difficult to remove. A common practice was to take the tree bark from the trunk to a point as high as a man could reach while the tree was still standing. As soon as the tree was felled, a swarm of eager hands quickly stripped the bark from all but the very smallest branches to complete the job. A variation on the theme was practised in the Forest of Dean. The extraordinary sight of the woodsmen of the Dean climbing ape-like through the crown of a great oak tree could still be seen in the forest until 1914.[18] Having shaved the bark off its upper branches and trunk with their special barking tools, the tree was left stark and lifeless until it was time to fell it in the preferred winter felling season.

It was the import of bark from the continent and its substitution by cheap tanning substances that put paid to its production in the second half of the nineteenth century. By this time, low-cost factory-made boots and shoes were coming onto the market, so ending the traditions of boot- and shoemaking as a village craft. James Brown, in *The Forester*, tells us that oak bark prices in Edinburgh, the main market place for tanbark in Scotland, dropped from £16 per ton to £5 10s between 1825 and 1850, so making (as he considered it) the working of coppices uneconomic.[19] In Wales, the Chepstow bark trade ended in the 1880s.

The production of charcoal and the growing and salvaging of tanbark can in many ways be seen as industrial processes, such was the large scale on which they were carried out. When it came to woodland crafts, however, the methods and means were more localised and varied, and almost every kind of tree had its own special uses. Herbert Edlin, a prolific and respected author on forestry and woodland topics in the middle years of the twentieth century, produced, in 1949, a well-illustrated book on *Woodland Crafts in Britain*, which explains and depicts the wood crafts in all their huge variety, from barrels to basket making, clogs to cricket bats and hurdles to hedging. Having evolved from the earliest times at the centre of the social and economic life of Britain, many of the wood crafts suffered from a rapid decline in the second half of the nineteenth century and the early twentieth.

An example of this decline can be drawn from the beech woods of the Chilterns, where the so-called 'bodgers' shared with the charcoal burners the doubtful pleasures of living as well as working in the woods. Living in makeshift huts and camps, they fashioned the legs, stretchers, spindles and sticks needed to make the old Windsor and Wheelback pattern chairs. In another of his books, *Trees, Woods and Man*, Edlin describes how he watched a beech tree being felled, cleft and turned into chair legs in a matter of minutes by one man using only hand tools and a primitive pole lathe worked by foot power.

Edlin, in the 1940s and '50s, had been fortunate to find one of the few remaining bodgers. When steam-driven machine tools arrived in the 1880s, the chair assembly yards had been turned into small factories, so opening the way to the use of imported timber. It is said that by around 1900 three-quarters of the timber used for chair-making in the Chilterns came from North America at half the price of the Chilterns beechwood. The fate of the bodgers is succinctly described in a 1919 *Report on Wages and Conditions of Employment in Agriculture*:

> Twenty to twenty-five years ago there might have been found one hundred men employed at Beaconsbottom, to take one village out of many as an example. In 1914 ... there were not ten men so employed ... As the big factories with their machinery cheapened production, the village craftsmen were driven to expedients to save costs, [converting] into second and third class material the tops of the trees which were left behind by the fellers working for the factories. There was hardly any money to be made at the business, however, and all the young men went to the factories and the boys ceased to learn the trades.[20]

To a large extent, this description of decline was emblematic of the demise of woodcraft more generally in all parts of the country, as village-made products were replaced by machined goods and people migrated from the woods to the factories in the towns.

Iron Ships and Taxes

The interesting story of the wood and timber markets is continued in Chapter 8, but mention must be made here of the moment that the building of wooden navy ships was brought to an end in favour of iron and steel, and when, as a consequence, the much-vaunted and historic market for large oak trees disappeared almost overnight. Iron-hulled ships had started to appear in the 1840s; Brunel's SS *Great Britain* — a steam-driven iron ship for transatlantic travel — was launched in 1845 and was twice the size of the largest wooden ship ever built. The Royal Navy's first experimental iron-hulled warship, the *Warrior*, was launched in 1860. A brief naval encounter in the American Civil War sealed the fate of the wooden warship.

In 1862, the protagonists faced each other off the coast of Norfolk, Virginia, with two experimental ironclads, the *Monitor* and *Merrimack*, the former on the Union side and the latter a Confederate ship, the *Merrimack* having earlier demolished two of the Union's wooden battleships, the *Congress* and the *Cumberland*. The battle, it seems, was inconclusive, but the lessons drawn from it were definitive. The performance of the iron ships astounded the naval authorities on both sides of the Atlantic. Although supposedly capable of destroying anything afloat, the wooden frigate was suddenly rendered obsolete and its proud dynasty consigned, rather igno-miniously, into history.

This pivotal event in naval history is often pictured as the ultimate catas-trophe for landowners. For centuries they had been encouraged to grow oak for the navy and suddenly it was no longer wanted. Whether the reality quite justifies this popular history is doubtful; its economic impact on land-owners was probably less than its psychological effect. Many landowners had preferred the shorter and potentially more lucrative cycle of coppice working to the infrequent and uncertain rewards of growing large trees for navy timber. Nevertheless, the collapse of this market, which was so much a talisman for Britain's seafaring supremacy, would have been a talking point at every county dinner table and would have served as nothing but a dis-couragement to the planting of trees.

A final blow to the financial health of the landowners must be added to this list of the woes of nineteenth-century woodland management. Estate duty was introduced by the short-lived Rosebery government at the modest level of 7 per cent in 1894, but was progressively increased in the following century to 40 per cent after the First World War, and to 60 per cent by 1939. For one thing it drove landowners, on inheriting property, to sell timber to pay the dues. As early as 1904, A.C. Forbes thought that death duty, in the few short years since its introduction, had done more to hinder the improvement of English woods than any single event in the nineteenth century: 'The first step ... was invariably that of cutting as much timber as possible including immature woods long before they ... are ripe.'[21]

It also discouraged replanting. The distinguished Edinburgh and Scottish architect Sir Robert Lorimer, writing in the magazine *Country Life* in 1916,[22] deplored its effects:

> It is obvious that a laird who is just able to keep his old family place, and who forsaw that his son [would] inevitably have to sell it, could not be expected to embark on a planting scheme from which there can be no return for 60 years if he plants softwood and for anything up to 300 years if he plants oak or other hardwood.

The news wasn't all bad, however. There was still one reason for landowners to look after their woods, and this was for sport. As estate woods became less important as producers of timber, they became more highly prized as coverts for game and as estate amenities. Shooting, between 1875 and the First World War, became the focus of the landowners' social life (see Picture 27), and foresters found that their work became subordinate to the cultivation of fur and feather. The gamekeepers enjoyed great freedoms; now it was they, not the foresters, who decided when a particular wood might be felled or a coppice-cut taken. This was resented by foresters and scorned by a growing band of forestry academics. Yet, realistically, shooting was good for woods; it reduced the pressure on landowners to fell trees prematurely for cash and it encouraged the protection of woods against damage from domestic stock or, worse, from the aspirations of the farm tenant looking to increase his acreage. Furthermore, shooting provided alternative work for some of the displaced estate workers as the traditional wood markets and coppice trades died out.

Development Pressures and Access to the Countryside

We are now comfortably in that part of the nineteenth century when the social trends that influenced forestry in the twentieth century came to the fore. One was people's appreciation of the countryside as an amenity, both for its beauty and for its pleasures as a place for outdoor recreation. There was no general law of public access to forests in Britain, so *common land* assumed a special value and importance. Most people valued commons not for the exercise of commoning rights such as the grazing of animals, but as places to walk and as a green and leafy contrast to the built-up cities and suburbs. The notion of day trips to the countryside also grew up in the latter part of the nineteenth century. The development of the railway system after the 1830s – a full 100 years before the ownership of cars became common – encouraged the pastime of hiking or, rather less energetically, the opportunity of a ramble in countryside that had previously been beyond the reach of the town-dweller. The railway companies laid on excursion trains to scenic spots like Betws-y-Coed in North Wales and to the Lake District.

Pressures to 'reclaim' areas of common land at the end of the eighteenth century, and into the nineteenth, were not just for farming, but for house-building too. Rodgers, in his book *The English Woodland*, tells us how William Chalmers, one of the eighteenth-century creators of the Kew Gardens, 'bewailed the fact that the New Forest was fulfilling no useful mission and that it contained thousands of charming sites for villas and thousands of acres of reclaimable land'. Rodgers goes on: 'It was the same thinking that, in 1871, led certain Southampton people to agitate for the parceling out of the forest into farms and smallholdings, the reclamation to be done with the aid of government loans.'[23] Pressure for the 'development' of the forest was mounting, so provoking opposition. In 1867, the New Forest Association was formed with the aim of preserving the natural beauty of the forest and pressing for legal action to protect the ornamental trees and woods. In 1877, a New Forest Act made provision for, among other things, the existing character of the scenery to be preserved.

Epping Forest stands out as one of the great causes célèbres in the struggle to protect common land from reclamation. Once part of the great Norman forest of Waltham, all that was left of Epping in the mid-nineteenth century was a tract of woodland joining the urban hinterland of London to what was then rural Essex, altogether about 6,000 acres of woodland and heath. It had become, in the words of its great historian William Addison: 'the Londoners paradise above all others, the gateway to green trees and grassy glades for thousands of dwellers on the east and north sides of London.'[24]

Our interest here is not so much in the forest itself, as in the first moves by people to agitate for and to be granted a right of access to woods, a theme with echoes in the twentieth century as we shall see in later chapters. Epping in the 1860s was owned by the 'lords of the manor' (various local squires and landed gentry) but was subject to ancient rights of common-ing, such as tree-lopping and the pasturing of animals. Addison explains how opposition to forest enclosure and 'disforestation' by the landlords had started in the 1840s, but found a real voice in 1866 when one Tom Willingdale with others was convicted of lopping trees and imprisoned. Willingdale could hardly have imagined the notoriety that his appar-ently routine conviction would provoke. Prompted by the newly founded Commons Preservation Society, and stirred up by public indignation over the conviction, the Corporation of London took up the cudgels to chal-lenge the legality of the enclosures and oppose 'disforestation'.

The result of a long struggle in the law courts was a court order to stop the enclosures and to have the newly erected enclosure fences taken down. The forest was saved for the people, and for the commoners too, although the latter's pleasure in the outcome was ultimately to turn sour. In the twen-tieth century, commoning in Epping was squeezed out of existence through the pressures of urbanisation; there were too many people, too much traffic and too many road deaths of commoners' livestock. But it was still a defini-tive campaigning victory for the general public where it most counted. The 1878 Epping Forest Act decreed that the forest's 'natural aspect' should be preserved for all time, remaining open and unenclosed for the enjoyment and recreation of the people: 'It gives me the greatest satisfaction to dedicate this beautiful forest to the enjoyment of my people for ever,' said Queen Victoria when she 'opened' the forest in May 1882.

A Depleted Inheritance

'The disproportionate spreading of tillage' is how John Evelyn, in the sev-enteenth century, explained the decline of woodland, little knowing that the losses would continue until the second half of the nineteenth century, when, with the agricultural recession, tree clearance quietened down. At the end of that century, a national census of woods suggested that the tree cover was, in total, just 1.1 million hectares[25] or about 5 per cent of the land surface of Britain, probably the low point of forest cover and when, as they say, 'records began'. A sort of statistical balance then existed. Around half the area comprised the fragmented remains of ancient woodland. The other half was *reforestation* – which is what this book is about. Most of this second half was the result of the energetic bouts of tree planting described in this chapter, on the whole what we now refer to as estate woodland.

Of course, a bald statistic of tree cover like this does not tell the whole story. It gives no feel for the magnificent variation of the British countryside or the soils, climate and human history that have shaped its tree landscape. But it is telling enough to convey a certain picture. In European terms, Britain was at the bottom of the league table for forest cover. And in the laissez-faire economics of the Victorian age, things could only get worse. To many people at the turn of the century – and particularly to the forestry enthusiasts – the case for reforestation must have seemed obvious.

2

VOICES FOR FORESTRY

It seems strange to read the exhortations of the nineteenth-century forestry campaigners written with the same degree of belief and passion as
environmental campaigners express for their own various causes today.
The story of the forestry movement starts with the founding of two arboricultural societies: the Scottish one in 1854, now the Royal Scottish Forestry
Society, and the English one in 1882, now the Royal Forestry Society of
England, Wales and Northern Ireland. The two societies – each formed
from a small nucleus of enthusiastic foresters and tree nurserymen – had
uncontroversial beginnings and modest aims. Their connections, of course,
were with the world of the private landed estates and their founding titles as
'arboricultural societies' reflect not the role of the arborist as we understand
it today, but the traditional arboricultural approach to their forestry activities that were practised by the landowners of that time.

When the Scottish society was granted royal patronage in 1869, it
reflected the growing involvement of the big Scottish landowners. Two
of the greatest landowners, Lord Rosebery and the Duke of Buccleuch,
joined in 1875 and 1879 respectively. 'Study and pursuit' was the nub of
its charter, but the new elite of wealthy members added ambition and
influence, so encouraging a more campaigning style. Voices for forestry could soon be heard beyond the members of the society itself. An
International Forestry Exhibition was organised in Edinburgh in 1884 to
promote education in forestry and to raise public awareness; it attracted
over half a million people in the course of its three-month run.[1] The
society's president, the Marquis of Lothian, complained that Britain was
the only European country without a School of Forestry, yet 'there is no

country whose future is so much bound up in the maintenance of woods as Britain and her colonies'.[2]

The development of the two societies can be followed in the business pages of their respective journals. As their memberships increased, they campaigned with greater persistence, urging the creation of forestry schools and the planting of 'demonstration forests'. Between the 1880s and 1914, the societies were involved in a long series of royal commissions and government enquiries that touched on aspects of forestry. An Agriculture Select Committee of the House of Commons in 1885 drew attention to the social and economic benefits of tree planting and recommended the establishment of a government Board of Forestry, a sort of parallel to the Board of Agriculture that had been established for farming. As might be expected, the various reviews were supported by landowning interests and, less obviously, by the import-oriented timber trade as well. A Board of Trade enquiry in 1902 concluded that 'indigenous forestry had been neglected', and proposed the introduction of educational and training initiatives in forestry skills, and that two areas of up to 10,000 acres each be cultivated for trees – one in Hampshire and the other near Edinburgh.

To be realistic, forestry, with its long time horizons, did not fit the economic laissez-faire of the times; the governments of the day were just not interested. Whatever was said about forestry, very little was actually done. When Lord Lovat opened the first British Empire Forestry Conference in 1920, he started on an apologetic note: 'We lead in one thing and one thing only – the number of Inquiries, Royal Commissions [and] Departmental Committees, which have examined and re-examined the forest situation in Great Britain, without, until 1919, doing anything effective to have it improved.'[3]

While the two societies agreed on many things, they had their differences too. The Scots were interested in afforestation (the planting of new forests on open land) while the English – to the extent that they had a collective view at this early stage – wanted to see an improvement in the quality of the existing woods. John Simpson, a consulting forester, complained in 1903:

> It is seldom anything of importance is said or written about forestry of which the text is not the millions of acres of waste land in Scotland and Ireland that might be planted; but although that plea may appeal to the State, it does not interest many owners of private estates whose woods demand all their attention. The waste lands needing attention first are the blank spaces in existing

woods, and which, in the majority of cases, are of greater extent than the ground occupied by trees. The fences are there but the crops are absent.[4]

Proposing a tree-planting programme against the background of what one expert had called a lot of 'blank spaces' did not seem a promising idea. The consultant's complaint needs some explanation, which will be covered fully in Chapter 4. In brief, though, starting in the 1880s, there was an infusion into Britain of forestry ideas and scientific principles from continental Europe. These notions, in turn, gave real credibility to the evidence that the societies and others put forward to the various reviews and commissions. They added technical theory and working principles to the societies' plans and proposals that would otherwise have been little more than guesswork.

So far the emphasis of the reviews and commissions had been on the timber side of forestry. Gradually, however, they turned to employment. The 1906 Royal Commission on Coast Erosion was set up in the first place to make recommendations about the encroachment of the sea in coastal areas. As a supplementary task, however, it was asked in 1908 to consider: 'Whether in connection with the reclaimed lands or otherwise, it is desirable to make an experiment in afforestation as a means of increasing employment during periods of depression in the labour market ...'[5] The Commission answered the question that had been posed with an unequivocal yes, and recommended no mere experiment either. It proposed, in 1909, the afforestation of an astonishing 9 million acres, of which 6 million were to be in Scotland, 2.5 million in England and 500,000 acres in Ireland. There was no mention of Wales which, for descriptive purposes, was often lumped in with England at that time. And it made clear that it was for the state to carry out the planting, pointing out the long time scales involved: 'If the state plants, it will certainly reap, which individual landowners can rarely hope to do.' It even speculated whether the implied land transfer to forestry should be assisted by compulsory purchase.

This seemed an ambitious proposal to the point of being reckless. Compulsory purchase was anathema to landowners and farmers felt threatened. The societies' forestry enthusiasts saw it as rash and untested, perhaps even harming their own more tentative and politically judged case for forestry. What they thought was missing was a practical social and land-use analysis – where was all this forestry to be 'fitted in' and what existing land interests would be displaced or otherwise affected? It was a ground-breaking proposal in the literal sense of the word too. The technical knowledge about methods of tree establishment on 'reclaimed' and marginal ground was limited at that time. True, the private estates in the nineteenth century knew something about tree establishment, but it would have been necessary to advance techniques well beyond the limits of the existing methods to implement the plan on the scale envisaged by the Royal Commission.

Lord Lovat: Soldier and Forester

One of the personalities in the Scottish society's council at this time was Simon Fraser, the sixteenth Lord Lovat, a man destined to play a key part in the future of forestry. Born in 1871, Lovat was a soldier who had inspired and recruited his own volunteer force, the Lovat Scouts, to fight in the Boer War in South Africa. Coming safely through the war, he took over the home estate at Beaufort, near Beauly in the north of Scotland, and occupied himself with its management and the tending of the woods that his father and grandfather had planted. He also got involved in public affairs in the Highlands, with various appointments in Inverness. His forestry interest was described by his friend and biographer Sir Francis Lindley to be 'an heredi- tary attribute'.[6]

Lovat's interest was much wider than that of technical forestry alone. His concern was for the social well-being of the Highlands, and he saw forestry as a *political* tool to arrest the drift of population from the villages and to diversify the failing economy. Lovat's aim was not to displace the crofter, but to strengthen the economy of crofting. He wanted crofters to supplement their incomes through subsidiary activities in the off-season and to extend and improve their holdings. Forestry, he thought, would provide jobs and create opportunities for the supply of services like tree nurseries and saw- mills. It seems that Lovat greeted the Royal Commission's report with a mixture of surprise and alarm, fearing it to be counterproductive. Not a man to rest on words alone, he decided to demonstrate the case for forestry in a more practical way. For that, he turned to his home area.

The Great Glen was the perfect study area for a forestry survey. It was typical in soils and climate of much of the Highlands, but had the great additional advantage of a ready-made route for timber extraction, the Caledonian Canal, which runs from Inverness on the Moray Firth to Fort William on the west coast. Although the landholdings in the region were very large, they were better known for their grouse and heather than for their agricultural potential. To help with the survey Lovat enlisted the help of his tenants and adjoining landowners. He set out to show how sheep farmers, smallholders and deer-stalking interests could all benefit from a well-designed and properly integrated forestry scheme. The report was published in 1911.[7] Its findings, as Lovat and his collaborators explained, showed how a state-aided scheme of afforestation could work and pay its way without major injury to existing interests, and would provide employment of a kind suited to the smallholders.

The societies, in the meantime, had been urging their campaigns on politicians in Westminster and Edinburgh. In March 1909, a delegation of members obtained a hearing from the Chancellor of the Exchequer, David Lloyd George, who was, it seems, a sympathetic listener. His 'People's Budget', presented later that year, provided funding for a newly formed Development Commission with powers to promote economic development and, amongst other things, 'the conducting of inquiries, experiments and research for the purpose of promoting forestry and teaching of methods of afforestation' and for 'the purchase and planting of land found after enquiry suitable for afforestation'.

After a slow and unpromising start, the Commission appointed a series of forestry advisors and offered financial help to encourage afforestation carried out by non-trading bodies like public authorities. The projects, however, were to be run on 'commercial principles'. For example, planting, in concert with popular fashion, took place in the catchments of a number of the new reservoirs being built to supply major cities, such as those of Lake Vyrnwy in North Wales (Liverpool Corporation) and the Talla reservoir near Edinburgh (Lanarkshire County Council). But all that ended when the First World War intervened and the work of the Development Commission came to a standstill.

Timber Wanted, but Forestry?

That a material as mundane as timber was vital for the war effort was perhaps less of a surprise to people in 1914 than it might seem to us today. Lloyd George's *War Memoirs* take up the story:

With the advent of war, the demand for timber grew considerably. Manufacture of armaments and munitions made an increased demand for

coal, and so for pit-props. The swelling torrent of supplies that poured overseas to our expeditionary forces called for an immense number of boxes,
including ammunitions boxes. If private building largely stopped, building of
factories, of army hutments, both here and in France, went on very rapidly,
and for this work wood was in chief demand. Trench warfare again involved
wood, as did railway construction behind the lines, with its call for innumer-
able sleepers, and there were miles of duckboards needed to cross the sodden
and shell-pocked areas. Wood, in short, was more than ever indispensable.[8]

Above all, wood was the vital raw material of the coal-mining industry
which fuelled the production of iron and steel. Steel, in turn, was needed
for almost everything: in the factories, the railways, and for weaponry and
shipbuilding. Pit props were needed in the mines in prodigious quantities:
deep mining was at its peak and wooden props were needed to shore up the
narrow underground passages that were typical of the coalfields throughout
Britain (see Picture 9).

What, in 1914, was not appreciated by the politicians was the dependency factor. At the outbreak of war, over 90 per cent of Britain's timber
needs were being met from overseas and the country was consuming about
half the world's total trade of forest products. The problem started to show
itself in the pages of the forestry journals. J. Milne-Home, writing in 1915,[9]
complained that no one had any idea that the collieries of England, Wales
and Scotland were almost wholly dependent on foreign supplies of pit
wood, while the Postmaster General expressed 'the greatest regret' that
British forestry had shown no interest in supplying the Post Office with
telegraph poles.[10]

Dependency, it seems, had led to complacency. The war was not expected
to last long and imported wood stocks in 1914 were high. Even so, the
home timber trade was unable to keep up with demand from the wartime economy. There were almost no statistics on domestic timber stocks or
on forestry, and only the sketchiest information on the home timber trade.
Meanwhile, the various parts of the industry – the sawmillers, timber hauliers, felling contractors and landowners – had little experience of working
together in a co-ordinated way. When imports from the usual supply countries in the Baltic region were cut off, the importers looked west to the
United States and Canada. But that was not the complete answer; German
U-boats were soon threatening the Atlantic routes too and timber imports
were taking up large amounts of much-needed shipping space.

By the end of 1916, the government's frustration with the slow pace of timber deliveries was boiling over. Imports were down and a quarter of the transatlantic shipping returning to Britain failed to arrive. In February 1917, Lloyd George (by then Prime Minister) remarked that timber absorbed more shipping than any other import and that if tonnage was to be saved for food and other imported goods, the problem of timber supply was the first one that had to be solved.[11]

We shall return to the story of Britain's wartime timber operations in Chapter 8. By 1918 the war was won and getting timber to the mines and the fighting front was said to have been a close-run thing. The official records – the result of landowner surveys after the war – suggest that 450,000 acres of woodland were cut down.[12] Even in comparison to the much larger forest industry that exists today (where felling and replanting amounts to about one-tenth of that area every year), it is a large area. E.C. Pulbrook in his *English Country Life and Work* remarked on the look of the landscape and the unusual urgency of the forestry work he saw:

> Settlements of log huts, more familiar to the backwoods of America than the ordered landscapes of England, sprang up in clearings and on hillsides, and coverts once sacred to the pheasant were transformed into deserts of mud mottled with tree stumps and mountains of sawdust. In alcoves formed of stacks of timber, saw [benches] driven by oil engines speedily converted trees into pit props and trench supports.[13]

The Man for the Job

To find Lovat at the beginning of the war, we have to go to the eastern Mediterranean where, reunited with his Lovat Scouts, he was involved in the ill-fated Dardanelles campaign. There he became ill with dysentery – a disease he had first contracted in the Boer War – which put an end to his front-line army service. When he returned to Britain at the end of 1915, he was disappointed and frustrated but, after convalescence, was ready for something new. Early in 1917, he was cajoled into taking over the management of the timber supply to the British army in France, being appointed there as 'Director of Forestry'. According to Lindley, it was not a task that Lovat sought or greatly welcomed after the excitement of front-line soldiering, but, as in all else, his energetic enthusiasm caught hold.[14]

It seems that the job was no sinecure, and today we can only marvel at the sheer scale of the resources he controlled. The aim of the directorate was to make the British army in France self-sufficient in timber, an undertaking with (as his biographer recalls) some unusual sensitivities. Negotiating with the often fickle French forest owners about the release of their standing timber for the war effort was a delicate process that required patience. Also, the Canadian timber units under his command could be perverse and difficult to manage, though his professional commitment to the job won them over. Lovat ended the war with responsibility for sixty-three Canadian forestry companies, eleven Royal Engineer units and a vast array of unskilled labour amounting in total to 45,000 men.[15] It might have crossed his mind – had he been aware of what was coming – that, compared to his responsibilities in France, the running of the still unformed Forestry Commission would be easy.

Sir Francis Acland: a Landowner at the Cusp of the Old and New

We now meet another familiar name in forestry, remembered for being chairman of the government committee that brought the Forestry Commission into being. Sir Francis Acland was the MP for Camborne and a substantial landowner in Devon and Somerset. His family held sway over the estates of Holnicote, at Selworthy on the northern fringes of Exmoor, and Killerton near Tiverton, both of them now National Trust properties. Like the Lovats, they had a keen family interest in trees – Sir Francis' grandfather, Sir Thomas Acland, had planted the woods above Selworthy section by section to commemorate the births of each of his ten children between 1809 and 1827. *A Devon Family* by Anne Acland tells the story of this family, a 'political' one of liberal inclinations. Francis Acland was born in 1874 and went into Parliament in 1906.

Lovat's war commitments in France did not prevent him from contributing to Acland's forestry committee. He travelled regularly to England and the two of them got on well, meeting at Killerton. We can picture them strolling on the lawns of the handsome tree-filled garden, there plotting the future shape of forestry. The gardens had been the creation of a then young and inexperienced Scots nurseryman and garden designer John Veitch (later a famous plantsman), who had developed them for Acland's great-grandfather in the 1770s. Even today, the gardens seem to be touched by the ghosts of Acland and Lovat. Many years later Acland wrote of his friend: 'he was my mental hero, and if I ever came across some bit of good dextrous work that helped things forward it was with the thought how this would please Lovat.'[16]

A little more about the political leanings of the Acland family will help to illuminate the background to the creation of the Forestry Commission, which Acland and his committee in due course recommended. His grandfather had been close to W.E. Gladstone in his student days in the late 1820s and was involved in Gladstone's 1868 government. The mood of the Liberal party was unsympathetic to landowning, and the *social* ownership of land – familiar today in various forms – had begun to surface as a new political idea, as instanced by the founding of the National Trust in 1893. Acland was, in a sense, a landowner caught between the old patrician way of doing things (the lifestyle of the patriarch of large rural estates) and the emerging new forces in landownership represented by the National Trust and the soon-to-be Forestry Commission.

That the Aclands were sympathetic to the trend of public ownership seems clear. In 1917 Sir Thomas Acland (a later generation Sir Thomas and Francis' uncle), then owner of the estate, gifted 8,000 acres of Exmoor to the National Trust. The story of this remarkable gift is recorded in *The Times* of 22 February 1917.[17] A letter from the Chairman of the Trust, the Earl of Plymouth, applauds Sir Thomas for his generous gift of 'very beautiful country' to the Trust. Overnight, it more than doubled the fledgling Trust's landholding and set the pattern for the National Trust's covenanting scheme which became popular in later years. There seems little doubt that Francis Acland was no mere spectator to his uncle's wishes in making this gift, but rather a quiet activist for whom the gift was a principled and instinctive act.

Acland's committee in 1916 was made up mostly of landowners sympathetic to forestry, so perhaps there was never much doubt about the outcome. Acland concluded that the nation's dependence on imported timber had proved a serious handicap to the conduct of the war and that 'The United Kingdom cannot run the risk of future wars without safeguarding its supplies of timber as every other Power that counts has already done'. He recommended a state-assisted programme of forestry that would make the country independent of imported timber for at least the duration of a three-year emergency period. As well as improving the productivity of the existing woods in the country, it meant the afforestation of 1.77 million acres over an eighty-year period, of which the committee wanted to see 200,000 acres planted in the first ten years.[18]

Furthermore, it proposed that the state should do the work directly: 'the State is not justified in asking private individuals to bear the burden', although 'the area to be planted by the State may be reduced in the same degree as private individuals come forward to do the work'. The committee recommended the setting up of a forestry authority (later called the Forestry Commission) 'equipped with funds and powers to survey, purchase, lease and plant land and generally to administer the areas required [and] to make limited grants for every acre replanted or newly afforested by public bodies or private individuals ... in accordance with approved plans and conditions'.

Just to be sure, the committee offered some other good reasons for planting trees: 'Afforestation would increase the productiveness and population of large areas of the British Isles which are now little better than waste ... but capable of growing first class coniferous timber of the same character of that imported.' They envisaged that the land could easily be found from rough grazings without reducing meat production by more than 1 per cent, while creating at least ten times more jobs than would be supported by the equivalent land area in agriculture. The committee's report, which was accepted by the Cabinet and published in 1918 with the blessing of all political parties, led to the Forestry Act of 1919 and the founding of the Forestry Commission.

This outcome was a triumph for the Scottish society. The recommendations were essentially a pre-war Scottish formula, remodelled to cover the wartime situation and emphasising not just the strategic importance of forestry, but the role that forestry could play in social terms in Britain. The English society was uncertain and divided in its deliberations.[19] Unsurprisingly, in the light of their earlier concerns, what they really wanted was financial support for *private* forestry; and what they feared was that state forestry might be a Trojan horse for land nationalisation. The ambivalence of the English landowners seems to have cast a shadow over the implementation of Acland's recommendations for the next twenty years or so, because the Forestry Commission paid little more than lip service to the landowning community and concentrated on the task of afforestation on behalf of the state (see Chapter 4).

The Forestry Act was, by any standard, a remarkable piece of legislation. The creation of a huge public land estate in Britain was the very antithesis of the free market economy that had prevailed since the 1850s. The under-lying argument for this 'special' treatment was that trees were not like the farming or manufacturing industry which could be geared up at short notice in response to meet a sudden demand. Rather, it needed a political commitment because it was a long-term investment with a planning hori-zon far beyond the life of any single government or individual landowner.

Constitutionally too, the Forestry Commission was unusual, being seen at that time as somewhere between an orthodox government department and the boards set up for running public utilities like the nineteenth-century Post Office, the BBC (1926) and later the electricity and various agricul-tural marketing boards.[20] It was not answerable to Parliament through any specific minister or Whitehall department, but had a quasi-independent board of Commissioners. One of these had to be a Member of Parliament in order to answer any questions about the work of the Commission in the House of Commons. The whole concept was hard fought for by Lovat against closeted departmental interests that wished to keep it 'in house' as a departmental service. It meant too, as he desperately wanted, that for-estry would be centrally administered for the whole of Great Britain, not fragmented into separate parts in England, Scotland and Wales. As a public service board working at arm's length from the government, he hoped to encourage a bold and enterprising approach, free from the day-to-day dis-tractions of departmental officials and ministers.

Undoubtedly the Commission quickly became a highly proactive body. If the measure of success was its physical achievement on the ground, few would argue that it was not well structured for its purpose. But if opera-tional freedoms were an organisational strength, they were also a weakness. The Commission's arm's length relationship with the government of the day meant that it was subject to the detailed supervision of the Treasury and to the latter's annual subventions of cash. This made it especially vulner-able to a financial squeeze. In 1937 it was described by Robson (see note 20) as having 'suffered from direct control and interference by Parliament and the Treasury'. And while its separation from mainstream government made it sure-footed and focused on action, it was seen by some of its crit-ics as insensitive to public opinion. When, in the 1930s, the Commission was challenged over its proposals for tree planting in the Lake District (see Chapter 3), it was isolated and without friends. We shall see later how the Commission was brought under the aegis of successive Ministers of Agriculture after the Second World War.

Another striking feature was that the founding Forestry Commissioners were all, with one exception, private landowners. This was surprising even in the context of 1919. As it was a public body, Lloyd George might have wanted the Commission to have a more diverse mix of members, as indeed happened later. But it was the landowners with their experience of growing trees who were thought to be best equipped to govern what was perceived then as a mostly technical and specialist body; rather an over-simplification, as it turned out.

Among the first Forestry Commissioners were Lovat, Acland, Lord Clinton (a Devonshire landowner) and Sir John Stirling Maxwell of Pollock (one of the founders of the National Trust for Scotland in the early 1930s) who will later emerge as a significant behind-the-scenes influence on the development of forestry. Specific Commissioners were named to represent the Scottish and Irish interests.[21]

A particularly significant appointment was that of Roy Robinson, an Australian who had been the secretary to Acland's committee. He became the Commission's first Technical Commissioner and Accounting Officer (and later its Chairman, see Chapter 3). Lovat's biographer Lindley reflected that under these men 'there was no fear of [the Commission's] liberty of action leading to anything but efficiency combined with strict economy'.[22] Plainly these were seen as the defining organisational needs of the time. The same author sees Lovat as a 'forceful character', while John McEwen (one of the Forestry Commission's first employees) offers a more ambiguous comment in his book *Who Owns Scotland*: 'However in the appointment of Lord Lovat as its first Chairman … landlords knew that in this able, arrogant domineering man they had someone in charge who … would see to it that, as a Government department, it would never over-reach itself and get out of hand.'[23]

Thus, against a background in which the whole rural economy had been seriously depressed for nearly half a century, the woods and forests in Britain became a matter of public policy rather than places of sole interest to their private owners. The Forestry Act of 1919, remarkable for its creation in the first place, gains even more significance from its durability for over ninety years. Its functions and its main organ, the Forestry Commission, still survive today, albeit within the framework of the devolved governments that now exist in Scotland and Wales.

The Forestry Commission: Up and Running

It has been estimated that a quarter of the land surface of Britain changed hands between 1918 and 1922.[24] If this remarkable statistic is true, it reflects the problems of landowners rather than the condition of agriculture, which benefited from the prosperity of its wartime boost until late 1921. During the war, farm rents had been fixed, high food prices had been guaranteed to increase food production and farm workers had enjoyed a minimum wage to encourage them to stay on the land.

The concerns of landowners were different from those of their tenant farmers and the farm workers. Unlike their tenants and employees, landowners received no direct benefit from the wartime surge in food prices. Many of the great estates had lost their sons and heirs in the war or were in financial difficulty and were having to reduce their bank borrowings. According to their family chronicles, the great landed families of the Aclands and Lovats were no exceptions to this trend. The disposal in 1917 of the first part of the Acland Estate to the National Trust has already been mentioned. Lovat too saw the slump coming, writing from France to his wife in 1918: 'As a class I can see none more vulnerable than the Highland landlord, that is why I started at once to cut timber and also why I am trying to sell land.'[25] There was a flood of estate sales throughout Britain, and thousands of farms were sold by their owners to their tenants. Farmers thought – misguidedly as it turned out – that this was a good time to buy. The result was a fragmentation of woodland ownership on an unprecedented scale. Because the woods, along with areas of 'unimproved' land surrounding the farms, were not usually part of a farm tenancy, such odd parcels of land were sold off piecemeal at distress prices to the highest bidder.

In late 1921 the farming economy also caught the cold. It was a return to the creed of free-trade politics and the end of price guarantees and wage controls that did it. The government, while persuaded of the case for funding forestry, decided on a general return to open-door economics in which agriculture was no exception. Food prices slumped as imports of grain and beef flooded in from all over the world. Many farmers, burdened by the mortgages they had so recently taken on, went bankrupt; a trend which lasted almost until the outbreak of the Second World War in 1939. This precipitated a renewed surge of population drift from the country to the towns. It was said that workers left the farming industry at the rate of 10,000 a year and that 4 million acres of arable land was either returned to pasture or left to become scrub.

These events created a climate in which an approach from the Forestry Commission must have seemed a godsend to many landowners, whether they needed the money to pay off their debts or merely thought that capital invested in the land was money wasted. Often it was the landowners who approached the Forestry Commission, and inevitably the Commission could pick and choose what to buy and when to walk away. The Commission wasted no time in a truly remarkable feat of land assembly. Its very first annual report to Parliament records the acquisition of land from the far north of Scotland to the south coast of England, and from the north-west corner of Wales to East Anglia.

The Commission did not have a free hand with its purchases. By the terms of Acland, it was committed to buying land of low value, either 'waste' or rough grazings that carried low numbers of sheep. A ceiling on what the Commission could pay was set by the Treasury; in 1922 the land price was set at £3 per acre and later at £4 per acre. Realistically, this meant that only land too poor for agriculture could be purchased: either acidic, sandy lowland heaths or land in the foothills of the uplands. Lovat and Robinson did not quarrel with the price constraints imposed on them because they wanted forestry to be looked at commercially; if it was going to survive, they reckoned that the lower the purchase price the better the financial return. The Commission's annual report for 1924 shows that it paid an average price of £3 8s 0d per acre for the land it bought during its first five years of existence. Moreover, the properties it bought for planting often came with other 'assets' thrown in – estate houses, farmland and unplantable mountain tops. Taking such extras out of the calculation, the Commission estimated that its *plantable* land had cost the taxpayer the equivalent of £1 15s 4d per acre.

How did the process of land assembly work in practice? Skipper and Williamson's little book on Thetford describes how the Commission built up one of its largest forests. During the agricultural depression of the 1870s, the Breckland of East Anglia had become a landscape of largely abandoned and derelict farms. Nothing grew and nothing thrived, except rabbits. When the Commission came on the scene in the 1920s, it was a distinctive area of large interlocking farms and private estates, partly composed of land improved for agriculture, partly planted with small woods and hedges and partly semi-natural grassland.

The sequence of land purchase and tree planting is described in detail in the book. By 1925 the forest comprised 20,000 acres and employed ninety-five people in the winter and forty-six in the summer. The best land was retained in agriculture: twenty smallholdings and small farms had been put in repair and a further twenty-seven holdings were under construction. By 1939 it comprised 59,000 acres. By that time the opportunity to extend the forest further was coming to an end. Agricultural methods made reclamation for farming both feasible and, at the beginning of the Second World War, the thing to do. The post-war Agriculture Act was intended to ensure that every acre of the Breckland that was 'improvable' was used for food production.

Almost as soon as land was acquired, tree planting began. Pines were favoured because they grew best on poor sandy soils and in regions of low rainfall. Because of their rapid growth, they were also more resistant than other species to the unseasonal frosts that were typical of the area. The young Scots pines were raised from seed collected from the wind-battered pine hedges that criss-crossed the old field areas, once planted as shelter for farm crops. Collecting seed from such dubious sources would be anathema to foresters today, who collect their seeds from vigorous trees of good form and appearance (see Picture 18) or from 'seed orchards' planted and designed for the purpose.

The other widely planted tree species was Corsican pine, a nineteenth-century introduction to Britain that had yet to make a mark in forestry. At Thetford it grew well in experiments and came to be regarded as the most productive tree, a point of view that lasted for seventy years but is nowadays being questioned. In the 1990s it became susceptible to a needle blight that causes dieback, thought to be exacerbated by the hotter summers experienced in recent years. No effective way of controlling the disease has yet been found.

The unpredictable sweep of disease had claimed a casualty with a more positive outcome for forestry in 1953. Rabbits were a major pest throughout Britain until the virulent strain of myxomatosis arrived. Rabbits devour young trees and chew the bark from older ones. At Thetford, 82,312 rabbits are said to have been taken from one typical planting area of 6,000 acres. Lovat, it seems, hated them, and his biographer noted that he took a personal interest in their removal: 'Rabbits, that scourge of foresters and agriculturists, were anathema to him. No excuse was accepted, and, if a trapper employed by the Forestry Commission did not keep the rabbits down, he went.' The result, we are told, was 'no serious trouble with rabbits even in the Eastern Counties'![26] That may have been an optimistic assessment by someone who didn't really know.

Culbin Forest, near the mouth of the River Findhorn in north-east Scotland, was another area where sandy soils and a dry climate suggested that the choice of tree species should be pines. The foresters' acquisition report at the time of its purchase in the 1920s pictured it as a vast area of shifting sands, and popular history has it that the Barony of Culbin was a rich area of farmland and orchards centred on a large mansion house until it was engulfed in a great sandstorm in 1694. Fact or fiction, the great accumulation of sand dunes at Culbin had become a looming threat to the rich adjoining arable land whenever a storm blew up.

The art of planting trees in 'mobile' sand dunes is often associated with the Landes on the Atlantic coast of France near Bordeaux, which in medieval times was overrun by sand that buried whole villages and farmed estates. Towards the end of the eighteenth century, the problem was so serious that a decision was taken to plant trees as a way of 'fixing' the sand and stopping its spread. It was a successful venture because the inland areas of the Landes were reoccupied to great advantage in the nineteenth century. Copying the methods of the Landes, the surface of the dunes at Culbin was fixed by the planting of marram grass − a tough long-stemmed grass that grows through sand and spreads by rhizomes. The trees were then planted into the established marram areas, the grass keeping the sand in place long enough for the trees to get their roots down. Another approach used was to fix the *slopes* of the dunes and some of the difficult flatter areas by 'thatching' them with conifer branch wood, into which the young trees were then planted.

The mountainous country of the Cowal peninsula of Argyllshire is a topographical contrast in every way with the low ground areas of the Breckland and the Moray Firth. The wet and relatively mild climate of the west coast of Scotland is good for trees, but its extreme windiness severely limits the area that can be planted. Wealthy industrialists in the second half of the nineteenth century were drawn to the Cowal area for its shooting and fishing, building mansion houses and establishing country estates there. But hard times followed for the estate owners when the First World War brought an end to the Edwardian golden era of sport.

One of the more unusual land acquisitions for forestry in Argyllshire was the 10,000-acre Benmore and Kilmun Estate, best known today for its arboretum at Benmore, now part of the Edinburgh Royal Botanic Gardens. It was unusual because it was *gifted* to the nation for the purpose of establishing a 'national demonstration forest'.[27] Harry Younger, following the death of his wife in 1921, had no appetite for living in the draughty Benmore house with all the problems of financing and staffing it. The adjoining Glenbranter property also suffered an eclipse as a private estate. Its owner, the music hall artist Sir Harry Lauder, sold it and moved away when his son was killed in the war. Other acquisitions for the forest followed in the 1920s and '30s — Ardgarten and parts of the Ardgoil, Drumsynie and Glenfinart Estates. By the time the Argyll Forest Park was established in 1935 (see Chapter 3), it was already a 58,000-acre area of open hill and young forest.

Another gift to the nation was Halton Wood overlooking Wendover in Buckinghamshire. Alfred de Rothschild presented his 'two valuable forests … as a free gift to the country', while writing to the Prime Minister in February 1917: 'I feel that I am hardly justified in troubling you with these lines when you are so overwhelmed with work … [but I am] most anxious to place at your entire disposal the woods which I possess on my Halton Estate.' It was a gift which Lloyd George gratefully accepted, his diary describing how 'before long the splendid slopes of beech forest … were laid low by Canadian lumber-jacks'.[28]

Recruitment – Hitting the Ground Running

Where did the Forestry Commission find its people? The Commissioners' first annual report tells us that its staff were 'improvised from the service of the crown woods, the advisory officers [from the Department of Agriculture] and from men with continental or Indian experience'. Foresters needed to be resourceful and self-motivated; within a few days they would find themselves in very remote places where they were responsible for recruiting forest workers, conjuring up tools and equipment, creating new nurseries for raising the young plants, and for planning and supervising the planting of a new forest.

John McEwen was one of the few people to record his memories of the recruitment experience, which he did in his book *A Life in Forestry*. He is remembered, however, not so much for his forestry career but as an activist and campaigner for land reform in Scotland, and as the author of the controversial 1977 book *Who Owns Scotland?* His political leanings are beyond us here but his forestry story alone provides an interesting snapshot of the changing times in his long life of nearly 105 years. After leaving school in 1904, at the age of 14, McEwen sought employment on private estates and in parks departments; at the age of 30 he applied for a job with the newly formed Forestry Commission. He was appointed in 1920 to take up responsibility for Monaughty Forest in Morayshire as a 'Grade 1 Forester'. Despite the many ups and downs with his new employer, which are described in his two books, his view of the Commission was clear: 'The formation of the Forestry Commission and the start of state forestry was the finest thing that ever happened in land-use in the UK.'[29]

McEwen remembered how in his very first year:

> I was told I had to get 500 acres planted up that year from scratch [when] there was not a man nor a tool in the place ... we cleared and drained the land and planted it up in regular sections of 50 acres, one after another. In the second year, we had to plant 600 acres.

McEwen's social conscience showed itself in a concern for the well being of his employees:

> I left four 30 acre 'compartments' unplanted, and built a rusky of rough branches big enough for 30 or 40 men. When the men came out on a stormy day I hated to send them back, as they had often come a long distance to their work, so they could shelter when necessary in the hut, and get part of a day's wages.[30]

Another Scot, Jim Shaw, was the central character of a popular book by Ian Naill, *The Forester*. Born in 1892 into a 'forestry' family, Shaw served an informal apprenticeship with his father on the Killearn Estate in Stirlingshire. Injury in the war saw him take up a civilian job with the Timber Control (see Chapter 8) in Presteigne, Radnorshire, where he was responsible for a group of 150 Portuguese volunteers drafted in to produce pit props: 'not a soft number for draftees from the army', as James Calder, the Director of the Timber Control, warned him. A number of briefly held positions after the war led Shaw to the Commission's Gwydr Forest in the Conwy Valley, where he was the forester in charge for the rest of his career.

To the extent that any one individual might have been typical of the Commission's recruits, Shaw, with his varied background, could be that man. He was, it seems, travelling a well-trodden path when he left Scotland to find a job south of the border. The southerly migration had seen the traditions and practices of the Scottish estates become commonplace in all parts of Britain. William Linnard, in his book on Welsh forestry,[31] lists a

sample of twenty estates in Wales that employed Scots foresters in the nineteenth century, while A.C. Forbes in his *English Estate Forestry* recounts that
it was 'as much the correct thing for an estate to have a Scotch forester as it
was for a nobleman's establishment to possess a French chef'.[32]

The recruitment of woodsmen (or 'forest workers' as they preferred to
be known in the Forestry Commission) was more problematic than that of
the foresters who supervised them. It depended on the availability of local
men and sometimes women too, who in most cases had no experience at
all of forest work. Shaw saw the inexperience of the 'small-holders, sheep
men and miners' at Gwydr as his greatest problem. In Scotland, McEwen's
responsibilities included a forest nursery (Altonside in Morayshire), where
in 1924 he grew 7 million young plants, employing eighty men and women
and, in the process, 'clearing out the Elgin Labour Exchange'.

George Ryle was another forester to leave behind a first-hand account
of the early days of the Commission's work. His last book, *Beating about the
Bush*, never saw the light of day as a published work, but a copy is retained in
the Forestry Commission's library.[33] In it he remembered how, in 1925, men
were recruited for forestry work from the Labour Exchange at Clipstone in
the Nottinghamshire coalfield:

> men reported for work in plenty at 7.30 in the morning on instructions from
> 'the Labour', but also returned to 'the Labour' soon after 9.30 in the morning
> to complain that the work was entirely unsuitable and the pay quite ridicu-
> lously inadequate. This process continued for a week or two but each morning
> a few men returned to give it a try and so a sizeable gang was built up.

Ryle had a great belief that things were always ordered for the best: he
goes on:

> it became clear at a very early stage that there is really a countryman beneath
> the pallid skin of almost any underground worker. It is the same in South Wales,
> Durham and in Kent. Perhaps in their dark subterranean working hours their
> bodies cry out for a release into the wild spaces which they could so seldom see.

One of the ways that the Commission tried to strengthen its often itinerant
workforce was by the creation of Forest Workers Holdings, a scheme with
its political origins in the 1890s when moves were made to encourage the
creation of agricultural smallholdings. This bubbled up again after the First

World War. The concept of the farming scheme was to provide the bottom rung of a farming ladder that would encourage men to stay in the countryside or return to it.

The forest scheme was intended to provide the employer with a stable core of men committed to a long-term future working in the forest, and willing and able to turn out at 'unsocial hours' for emergencies or fire duty. H.A. Pritchard, a feisty Welshman who headed up the task of land acquisition in England and Wales, had a clear vision of what was intended:

> I have great hopes of seeing, at any rate in the Eastern counties, and particularly in our own Welsh areas, every ruined holding with its bracken-invaded pastures and derelict arable fields once more inhabited and with thriving families remaining on the land, with ample work and means to satisfy all their reasonable requirements. A population, strong, sturdy and independent, with a love of the land and a love of the forest deeply implanted in their nature.[34]

The holdings were not large enough to be fully self-supporting. The tenants were guaranteed a minimum of 150 days work in the forest each year, so dividing their time between forestry and small-scale farming. On the holding the tenants were free to grow crops, produce milk or raise stock, pigs and poultry. At Thetford they established a co-operative marketing scheme; poultry, eggs and honey were sent 'direct to the consumers in London at prices lower than those prevailing there but considerably better than those obtained locally'.[35] Sometimes the smallholders would keep horses to hire to their employer for ploughing or transporting materials. The holdings were meant to be a maximum of 10 acres by Treasury edict, but were sometimes larger. At first they were converted from derelict shepherds' cottages and outbuildings taken over by the Commission when they bought land, but later they were built specifically for the purpose.

Special care was taken in the recruitment of families for the smallholdings. Ryle, in another of his recollections, tells how the holdings in South Wales were sought after both by country folk from the neighbourhood and by ex-coal miners and industrial workers from further afield:

> At first we had grave doubts about these last and asked ourselves whether men and their families, brought up in the tightly knit communities of the mining valleys or the industrial north, would be able to acclimatise themselves to the remote hills and the hardships of outdoor work in all weathers.

We wondered how mum would take to minding a few cows, pigs and poultry while dad was up in the plantations all day and the children were away down the lane in a strange village school. There were misfits, but the selection of tenants was always meticulous.[36]

Visits were paid to the Labour Exchanges in Rhonda, Taf and Ebbw, where interested miners, to test their commitment and attitude, were told of the hardships and isolation of life as woodsmen. Ryle goes on: 'Then, without prior arrangement, each was visited in his home. There were spotless shining homes and slovenly homes. There were back gardens replete with leeks, spuds and cabbages and there were others barren or full of junk ... which decided us on our final selections.' The people from the towns, he said, 'quickly adapted to become the same good countrymen which, in all probability, their forebears had been a mere two or three generations earlier'.[37]

Money Worries

It is often true that commitments made in a crisis are forgotten when normal life resumes. That the Commission survived the downturn of the economy in 1921 was, it seems, more to do with its capacity for creating employment in rural areas than with any hard political conviction about its main purpose, so recently approved by Parliament. The so-called Geddes Axe was applied to many aspects of public expenditure, and the Commission was not alone in facing a challenge to its survival. Newspapers of the time pointed out that the squeeze on public expenditure represented an abandonment of *most* of the post-war 'reconstruction' promises. The Treasury in 1921 proposed that the afforestation programme would be scrapped. It imposed budgetary cuts on the Commission and suspended its authority to buy land. But the embargo on tree planting was lifted six months later when extra finance was provided for a job-creation programme!

With a distinct air of relief, the Commission's annual report for its second year reads:

The Commissioners regret the delay in the presentation of their second annual report. At the time when the report was due to be prepared the whole future of state forestry was in the melting pot and they were engaged in presenting afresh the national need for a forest policy. In the circumstances they felt it less urgent to report progress than to ensure that there should be progress to report.

The Commission's regular employees hated job-creation programmes because they saw them as a threat to their own employment. The Commissioners were in two minds; on the one hand, they welcomed the political support and extra funding it provided, but on the other, they deplored the distraction from what they saw as their real business of forest creation. So the Commission worked hard to dispel the fears of its employees, reassuring them that the job-creation work was of a kind that would not encroach on their own normal work.

Two other job creation schemes had an impact on forests in the interwar years. The Ministry of Labour's work camps, recently pictured by the BBC as the 'hidden labour camps of the 1930s', were sited in remote forests (as they must have seemed in those days) with the aim of providing redundant miners and factory workers with training in manual skills. The scheme ran from 1928 to 1939 and mostly involved forest road-building – a labour-intensive manual task in those days and a questionable investment since the timber extraction they were needed for would not occur for many years to come. The Special Areas Scheme was the other case in point; beginning in 1934, it provided extra funding for land purchases for forestry within the depressed regions of coal mining and heavy industry in South Wales, Tyneside, West Cumberland and parts of Clydeside and industrial Scotland.

The Crown Woods

In 1924 the crown woods were formally added to the Forestry Commission's fast-expanding landholding. A strangely diverse group of forests, they were 'inherited' from the rather mysterious Department of Woods, Forests and Land Revenues, and the Office of Woods within it. Some were the unlikely survivors of the early Victorian pressures to enclose and 'disforest' crown land, others the rumps of 'successful' privatisations in former times, and others again were recent acquisitions by the crown which included areas of bare land for afforestation. Of the 'forest' area of 120,000 acres of crown land transferred to the Commission, by far the largest were the historic New Forest and the Forest of Dean, two small remnants of medieval England. That they had out-lasted the pressures to 'disforest' them was because they contained a residue of oak trees suitable for the navy. And when the naval shipyards went into decline in the second half of the nineteenth century, they were saved again, this time because of growing public resistance to the whole idea of their privatisation and 'reclamation' for farming or residential house-building.

But what had motivated the department's uncharacteristic interest in the purchase of land for afforestation? Could it have been a response to the contemporary lobbying for demonstration forests and the desire to show willing in the new climate of interest in forest management? Perversely though, the new developments were situated in the most inaccessible places. In 1883, the department acquired and planted land on the Isle of Man where it had mineral interests (an area omitted from the transfer of forests to the Commission) and in 1899 it bought hill land for planting at Hafod Fawr near Penrhyndeudraeth in North Wales. The acquisition of run-down sheep farms at Inverliever in Argyllshire then followed in 1907; in those days Inverliever could only be reached by boat!

There was also evidence of a more responsive Department of Woods when, in 1904, a forestry school was established in the Forest of Dean for the 'systematic instruction of working foresters and woodmen'. In 1912, it moved to a converted factory site at Parkend, still keenly remembered today by some of its later 'graduates'. According to one former trainee: 'Not even the virginia creeper that covered it … could disguise its stark functionalism.'[38] But the training it gave was good, as one school graduate ventured: 'no one in my time could complain that he had not had an acquaintance with the basic trinity of planting, weeding and felling.' The educational picture for forestry, so long campaigned for by the two societies, was completed with the founding of degree courses in forestry, the first at Bangor University in North Wales in 1907[39] and others in Aberdeen, Edinburgh and Oxford in the 1920s. Parkend, in 1919, became the first of the Forestry Commission's training schools. And in 1926, the Society of Foresters of Great Britain (now the Institute of Chartered Foresters) was formed to 'advance and spread in Great Britain the knowledge of technical forestry in all its aspects'.

The Founding Father

It is impossible to separate the shape of early twentieth-century forestry from the character and background of Lord Lovat (see Picture 5). Forestry in 1919 meant, to all intents and purposes, the Forestry Commission; there was no organised and effective private forest sector and his lordship seems to have been happy with it that way. His landowning background convinced him that a different form of land stewardship – afforestation by the state and the creation of a dedicated agency to do it – would be needed if real progress was to be made. His qualifications for running the Commission were unique. He knew from his involvement in public affairs in the Highlands what political and social challenges would be thrown up. His testing background in the army and in France had equipped him with unique organisational skills. Finally, he was well connected and 'a master of tact and diplomacy', able to use his influence when the Acland proposals looked set to falter in the scrum of post-war departmental politics or because the economy was going through hard times. By the time Lovat retired in 1927, the Commission had assembled and planted 45,000 acres in more than 100 different forests, and employed 2,735 people. He died in February 1933.

3

THE IDEAL PLACE TO
GROW TREES

The interwar years have a bad reputation. Unemployment was the great political problem of the day. By the end of the 1920s nearly 3 million people were out of work. The depressed economy reflected the decline of heavy industries like coal and steel, and the cold winds of Britain's return to free trade. By 1929, most of the world had fallen into a recession which continued to deepen. As we saw in Chapter 2, the disillusionment and financial problems of landowners and tenant farmers after the war led to a flurry of land sales, and many acres of arable land were converted to pasture or allowed to revert to scrub.

During the period 1932–52, Roy Robinson, an Australian, was the Chairman of the Forestry Commission. His was an unusual appointment because, to all practical effect, he combined the post of Chairman with that of general manager. This was a period of both consolidation and 'scripting' for the newly established Commission, albeit with the setback of another terrible war.

Robinson Rules

Roy Lister Robinson was born on 8 March 1883 in Macclesfield, Adelaide, South Australia. Twelve years younger than Lovat, he came to Magdalen College, Oxford, in 1905 as a graduate mining engineer and Rhodes Scholar to study natural sciences, including geology and forestry. In 1909 he was recruited by the Board of Agriculture and Fisheries and appointed to head up a joint forestry unit in which the Board, together with the Department of Woods (see Chapter 2), worked to breathe new life into the management of the crown woods. This was Robinson's introduction to practical forestry and his springboard to the Acland Committee. He became its secretary and, along with two of its members, Lovat and Stirling Maxwell, was a principal author of the committee's report.[1] Plainly he did well and, with all the right connections, stood out as the man to lead the new Commission. In 1919, at the age of 36, he was appointed as its first Technical Commissioner, serving under its appointed Chairman, Lord Lovat. In 1932 Robinson was himself appointed as the Commission's Chairman.

It was to be expected, from Robinson's all-embracing role, that he would be a good strategist and communicator. But he was also a very practical man, liking nothing better than to spend a day in the woods (mostly very young at that stage!) where he took a keen interest in the technical challenges of tree growing every step of the way. One of his first actions in 1919 was to set up a small research division to investigate the growing of trees on poor upland soils. Since his early days with the Board of Agriculture, he had had his eye on the North Tyne district of Northumberland. It was a vast, largely uninhabited upland, once described as England's empty quarter and, according to the official guidebook, a 'molinia prairie [having] developed for the most part a vegetation which was not even useful for sheep'. The climate of the North Tyne uplands was harsh and the soils were cold and unforgiving. Foresters observed that the climate there benefited neither from the milder conditions of the western uplands nor the comparative shelter of Britain's other eastern hills. But, with a sparse human population, it must have seemed the ideal place to grow trees. Two of the first land acquisitions there were at Newcastleton (on the Scottish side of the border) and Smales Farm at Falstone, the latter becoming an experimental forest.

In some ways, it would not be an exaggeration to describe *every* upland forest of those times as an experiment or at least as a 'learn as you go' situation. The science of growing trees on land stripped of its natural tree cover many centuries ago and degraded for generations by sheep and periodic burning had to be worked out from scratch. Robinson had been introduced to the Belgian turf-planting method by Stirling Maxwell, who had experimented with different methods of planting trees on peat at his estate at Corrour, Inverness-shire. So called because it was practised in the Belgian Ardennes, the method involved digging drains (by hand) at 20ft intervals across the ground, cutting and turning over the turfs and then distributing them across the ground surface to the tree-planting positions.

When the method was introduced at Falstone, it was a big breakthrough. The timing was perfect, coinciding as it did with some of the biggest land acquisitions. In 1932, the Duke of Northumberland offered to sell the Commission his 19,000-acre Kielder Estate, centred on Kielder Castle, a former shooting lodge.

If the theory of the turf-planting method was simple, the practicalities were rather more challenging when carried out on the scale of many hundreds of acres. The knack was to plant the trees *through* the turf, not into it. This channelled the roots of the young trees into a good growing medium where nutrition was provided by the decomposing grass and moss sandwiched between the turf and the original ground surface. It also reduced waterlogging by giving the young plants a slightly raised planting position.

At Falstone the men worked across the ground using a 'rutter'. This can best be described as a very large rounded spade designed to cut out the wedges of turf. One apprehensive recruit found there was a knack to it:

> my first impression of the cumbersome looking rutting spade was of disbelief that I should ever be able to effectively handle such an unwieldy tool. Even carrying it up onto the hill seemed to be a daunting prospect. After a few back-breaking days of slithering about ... and at the risk of slicing off some of my toes, I gradually managed to achieve some sort of working rhythm. I found that, as with many hand tools, once a knack had been acquired I was able to produce a reasonably acceptable turf.[2]

While the use of hand tools did the job in the wet, soft ground at Kielder, they were not strong enough for the hard and stony soils of the North York Moors, where tree planting also started in the 1920s. The moor had seen one of the first attempts at forestry ploughing in 1872, when 70 acres were ploughed up with a team of six horses – an achievement which won the contractor a 'Medium Gold Medal' from the Highland and Agricultural Society of Scotland.[3] But forestry ploughing was slow to take off because the equipment then available was too light and the costs too great.

Only with the import of the early types of tracked tractor from America in the 1930s did ploughing become an economic reality, and not until the early 1940s was a plough invented that could break *right through* the compacted layers of the heathland soils. This was the 'RLR', named after Robinson himself. Furrows were cut at intervals, mimicking the manual method of turf planting described above, and trees were planted in the ribbon of turf thrown up by the plough. Line ploughing like this was, of course, more economical than complete ploughing, saving time and money. Robinson is said to have been wary of experimenting with complete ploughing because he feared that it might invite an agricultural takeover of the ground. The power of the new machines opened up a world of possibilities for foresters. The young trees benefited from better drainage and nutrition and, because the machines were less dependent on the weather, ploughing could be carried out at almost any time of year.

Burning the Mountain

Another preoccupation of foresters in the early days was forest fire. Set against smoke-blackened landscapes on the grand scale of California or the Mediterranean region, forest fires in Britain do seem a fairly tame affair. Fires kill trees but, happily, in Britain they seldom threaten life and limb. The early spring is the time when it all happens as the previous season's now dead grass, fanned by capricious easterly winds, can be tinder-dry. Fire running through the grass and ground vegetation of a newly planted wood reduces it to a charred and blackened waste in only a few minutes, destroying years of work.

Notorious for their fiery nature were the forests of the coalfield region of South Wales, part of the huge Morgannwg Forest (now Coed y Cymoedd). The coalfield had not looked promising for forestry in the 1920s. The valleys were gloomy places suffering from economic depression, made worse by fumes from smouldering pit heaps and dust from the ongoing coaling activities blowing in the wind. The prospects for tree growth were made all the more difficult by atmospheric pollution. The forests of the Rhonda fringed the closed-in valley floors, even reaching to the ends of the gardens of miners' cottages, almost an invitation, it seemed, for carelessly dropped cigarette ends to start a conflagration.

The fires approached from the mountaintops too. It was the custom of the Welsh farmers to 'burn the mountain' to encourage an early bite for the sheep in the spring. At Margam, in the spring of 1929, all of the first two years' plantings (over 600 acres) were destroyed by a fire spreading into the forest from adjoining hill ground. A typical spring season in the valleys might see between 80 and 100 outbreaks, and many more 'call-outs' to neighbours' hill farms to defend the forest boundaries. Irrespective of the weather conditions, no holidays at all were granted to the forest staff for the whole of the fire danger period from February to May.

Fire was a preoccupation of foresters everywhere, not just in South Wales. In the flat-ground forests like Thetford, it was difficult to spot fires from a distance and so tall look-out towers were erected at the intersection of long, straight forest rides, sometimes laid out in a radial arrangement for ease of viewing. Communications were a 'Heath Robinson' affair. The towers were equipped with ex-army telephones linked together with miles of sagging cable which was constantly getting snagged and broken. Firewatchers had to separate any intertwined wires to stop them from shorting. Railway fires were another common hazard in forest areas. In the twenty years from 1929, railways caused 54 per cent of the 12,412 fires that were reported. Strips of land were ploughed up on each side of the line to swallow up sparks from the engines before they could ignite the dry grass vegetation in planted areas.

Landowners got no compensation for their ruined young woods, finding out to their dismay that the Railways Fires Act of 1905 limited the damages they could claim to a nominal amount unless negligence were proved. On spotting a fire, engine drivers were under instructions to raise the alarm by giving 'one crow, one long and one crow whistle' and to repeat the signal when passing the next station or signal box.[4] A patrolman would be on the spot to watch the railway line after a train had gone through. In Gwydr Forest in North Wales, one firefighter described how the steam engines produced 'myriads of sparks' when stoked for the steep gradient in the Lledr Valley:

> There were alarms and counter-alarms, smoke wisps here and smoke spirals there and the blaze would creep and curl, and then sweep up the boulder-strewn slopes and into the plantations, perspiring patrolmen in pursuit, beating at the flanks with their birch brooms, barking shins and arms on the heather and gorse-clad rocks. It was no fun.[5]

Only in the 1960s and '70s did the dangers of forest fire decline. Spark-arresters were fitted to steam engines in the 1950s and by then fire fighting was becoming easier due to better roads and because the new forests were becoming more varied in structure.

Landscape and the Lake District

If the Commission was getting to grips with its technical problems in the interwar years, it was still a beginner at dealing with matters of a more subjective and political kind. One of the most contentious aspects of afforestation was the visual change it imposed on upland landscapes. So when, in 1934, the Commission was offered for purchase the 7,243-acre Eskdale and Dunnerdale Estate in the Lake District, it was almost bound to arouse strong feelings. We are here at a time before the creation of the National Park, but the designation of the Lake District in 1951 made little difference to what was already a famous and cherished landscape. So started the dispute that was the Commission's first real taste of opposition to its work.

Tree-planting proposals did not come completely out of the blue to the Lake District. Villages like Ambleside and Windermere have a distinctly Victorian feel about them for the conifers growing in gardens and public places, and the nineteenth century saw the afforestation of several water catchments and the planting of shelter 'blocks' for wintering livestock. The surrounds of Tarn Hows, for instance – nowadays a noted beauty spot owned by the National Trust (see Picture 23) – were planted with Scots pine, larch and Douglas fir when the dam was built in 1865, and the Manchester Corporation planted pines and beeches at Thirlmere in 1909. The Forestry Commission added to this existing inheritance of mainly functional new woods in the 1920s and '30s when it planted its Ennerdale and Grizedale Forests.

In terms of extent, the dispute was not what it first seemed. By far the greater part of the estate – at least 5,000 acres – was too exposed and rocky to be planted, and right from the beginning, in 1935, the Commission agreed with the Friends of the Lake District that it would not plant trees on the rugged open landscape of the central fells, an area of 300 square miles. Outside this heartland, the Commission undertook to consult the Friends before buying land or planting trees in certain mapped areas that were also seen as sensitive landscapes. This brought in part of Eskdale, which became the main focus of the objections to planting. The Friends argued that the planting would completely ruin the glaciated wilderness character of the valley and displace the Herdwick sheep on which the local economy depended.

What started as a local campaign in opposition to the Eskdale tree planting broadened into an issue of almost national proportions. Famously led by the Reverend H.H. Symonds,[6] the campaign had escalated by April 1936 to the level of a debate in the House of Lords and prompted a huge flurry of correspondence in *The Times*. Thirteen thousand people, including many public figures, signed a petition against the mooted afforestation and the Archbishop of York, leading a delegation of petitioners to see Robinson that June, thought it 'doubtful whether so great a volume of feeling so deep has ever before been called forth in England by any aesthetic question'. Having made their voice heard, the Friends could do no more than wait, and the dispute rumbled on through the years of the Second World War. Only in 1943 did the Commission agree to give up its plans for planting trees in Eskdale. It was a great victory for the protestors.

If it seems particularly outrageous that the Commission should have contemplated planting in such a sensitive part of the Lakes, we might wonder why that was. Robinson was caught in two minds. The First World War had cast a long shadow and, seventeen years on, his memories of the Acland remit were still very clear. The Commission, he said, could not refrain from planting without prejudicing the task set to them by the government. More specifically, there were employment pressures to consider. The government was actively encouraging the Commission to buy land to relieve unemployment in the Special Areas (see Chapter 2), and the land in question fell within the orbit of the Cumberland Special Area. In 1936 alone the Commission was asked to arrange for the afforestation of 200,000 acres in the Special Areas.[7] Behind the scenes, Robinson pondered with his colleagues whether the Commission should withdraw from the Lake District completely, and argued that it had reached the stage in its development when it 'must not merely be reasonable, but must demonstrate the fact'.[8] But the lesson of the Lake District was clear; it was no longer possible to doubt that the beauty of the landscape would be a critical issue for forestry in the years to come.

Forest Parks

The afforestation proposal was not the only perceived threat to the character and landscape of the Lake District in the 1930s. Farmers and hill-walking groups were worried about the growing pressure of human feet on the fragile hills and, in common with beauty spots everywhere, the threats being posed by the ever-increasing advance of the motor car into the countryside (see Picture 28). Car manufacture in Britain had become a major industry

– one of the few bright spots in a gloomy economy – with output rising from 32,000 in 1920 to 182,000 in 1929, and the car became central to the whole idea of exploring the countryside. The preservationist cause was reflected in the establishment of the Council for the Protection of Rural England (CPRE) in 1926, with its sister bodies in Scotland and Wales, while the growing interest in recreational access to land saw the formation of the Youth Hostels Association in 1930 and the Ramblers in 1935.

Today, when hill farmers are being actively encouraged to develop tourism, it is a little hard to understand why the pressure for access to the hills created such a sense of conflict. Amidst the hardships and gloom of the economic recession, it seems incongruous that the issue came to the fore when it did. Town dwellers, faced with fenced-off countryside and a lack of roadside facilities for stops and parking, felt unwelcome and even threatened. Recognised rights of way were few and their use was actively discouraged. Landowners, for their part, were defensive, believing that the vogue for 'preservation' and public access were deterrents to productive farming, and feeling that their way of life could be overwhelmed by force of numbers. Tellingly, one contemporary observer was more optimistic:

> But an intelligent townsman will join with the countryman in resenting the degradation of our rural population to the status of lackeys who minister to the holiday requirements of the motorists; instead he will take pleasure in studying the skilful pursuit of rural occupations and the efficient management of land.[9]

A contemporary development was the National Parks idea, still no more than a vague and unshaped concept in the 1930s. In 1929, Prime Minister Ramsay MacDonald set up a committee under Dr Christopher Addison MP (later Lord Addison) to investigate the need for National Parks with a view to putting the best areas of the countryside out of reach of development and improving access for the public on foot. The Forestry Commission, in the meantime, was contemplating the idea of National *Forest* Parks, nowadays simply referred to as Forest Parks. Powers granted to it in 1927 enabled the Commission to introduce by-laws to 'control' public access and discourage irresponsible wild camping and fire-lighting. The Forest Park idea was to designate areas of fine scenery where the public could roam at will, helped by access tracks and campsites. There was, of course, an element of expediency about all this as it was putting to good use areas of mountain land that were too high up to be planted with trees. But that was coupled with real enthusiasm for the idea as well, notably from Stirling Maxwell.

Where Addison failed in his early quest for National Parks, the Forestry Commission was more successful in advancing its own scheme. John Sheail's researches in the Public Records Office (described in his *Rural Conservation in Inter-War Britain*) tell the story.[10] In 1933 Robinson put forward the idea of National Forest Parks in a memo to Prime Minister Ramsay MacDonald. This provoked a response from the Treasury which strongly objected to 'converting the Commission appointed to re-afforest Great Britain into an agency for promoting hiking'. It sought the views of the Treasury solicitor as to whether the Commission had the statutory powers that it would need for the purpose.

Ramsay MacDonald asked the Treasury to think again about the proposal. He thought it would be:

> tremendously popular and would perhaps be the best way of regulating a habit [hiking] which, hitherto, has grown up in a very disorganised way and unless carefully controlled may be a danger to public health and a serious blot on some of the most beautiful parts of the countryside ... sooner or later, especially when the flood spreads over desirable country like, for instance, the Cairngorms, something must be done, otherwise by fires and less disastrous incidents the countryside will be devastated except in very remote parts.

Eventually persuaded on the point, the Treasury had a profound change of heart while looking over its shoulder at the growing public support for the Addison plan. They began to see Forest Parks as a way of stalling the pressure for National Parks. They now suggested that there was nothing to stop the Commission providing reasonable access and modest facilities if it could be done alongside its 'proper work'. The Treasury told the Commission that the public could be offered reasonable access to its woods; that direction posts could be erected on trails; and that camping sites could be provided, all on the understanding that the public would be under 'proper control'. A sideline on the idea was the Treasury's proposal that volunteer bodies would be made responsible for the supervision of visitors and for providing huts and tents, though no more was heard of this.

It was with this encouragement from the Treasury and a grant of £5,000 that the Commission, in 1935, set up its first Forest Park in the hills of the Cowal peninsula of Argyll. The location had many natural advantages, dissected as it was by the sea lochs, Loch Long, Loch Goil and the Holy Loch, and the freshwater Loch Eck. It contained two campsites, a local beauty spot known as Puck's Glen and the much-visited gardens at Benmore close to Dunoon. A new visitor centre for the public was built in the empty Ardgarten House, and five youth hostels and four campsites were opened.

The public's positive response to the park and the demand for its facilities persuaded the Commission to create others. One was in Snowdonia, centred on Gwydr Forest and a new campsite that was established at nearby Beddgelert. The other was the Forest of Dean in Gloucestershire, already a well-established recreational venue. The Dean differed from others – and from those created immediately after the war – in being lowland in character and predominantly composed of broadleaved woodland rather than conifers. Its designation as a Forest Park was accompanied by the development of a camping ground at Christchurch. Improvements were made to the already popular Symonds Yat viewpoint above the River Wye – later to become a well-known spot for viewing peregrines – and to several picnic sites. But the work ended abruptly when the outbreak of the Second World War brought tourism to a juddering halt.

War Again

It must have seemed incredible in 1939 that the whole thing was about to happen again. When Britain's main softwood supply areas – the pine and spruce forests of the Baltic region – were cut off in the spring of 1940, followed by the drying-up of supplies from mainland Europe, wood production in Britain once again became a political issue. This time the government had the advantage of the lessons learned a generation earlier. No time was lost. From the outset, it took control of raw material supply and arrangements for timber imports were once again made with Canada. When the Atlantic supply lines were again threatened by submarines, timber cargoes were rationed to give priority to less bulky commodities.

Pit wood production was the greatest priority, as it had been in the First World War. In August 1942, Gerald Lenanton, the Director of Home Timber Production, wrote to the Royal Forestry Society appealing to its members for an increase in production:

> the shipping situation makes it absolutely essential that our home production
> of timber should be speeded up still further ... While all kinds of utilizable

timber are in demand, the most urgent need is for pitwood ... I know that
pitwood production entails the sacrifice of young plantations ... but the
maintenance of supply for the pits is of vital importance.[11]

There were many interesting demands for other kinds of wood besides the
need for bulk softwood for the pits. Birch and sycamore were once again
needed for factory rollers and cotton reels. Poplar replaced the imported
aspen used for making matches. Home-grown ash was used for tool han-
dles in lieu of American ash and hickory. Oak and larch were used in the
construction of small naval craft. Beech was made into rifle butts instead of
American walnut. Sweet chestnut palings found a new use as landing mats
for the tanks and heavy vehicles used in the Normandy landings, whilst
charcoal was needed in large quantities for chemical works and making
explosives. The countryside was scoured for the especially good grades of
ash and beech trees that were needed for aircraft manufacture. The use of
timber for aircraft construction had all but ceased after the First World War,
but it was in demand again for the construction of the all-wood Mosquito:
the ash was used for the airframes and the beech for making the plywood
veneers used for the 'skins'.

The story of the mobilisation of people for timber work is told in Chapter
8 but here our interest is in government policy and how the scarred landscape of felled woods created a new political mandate for forestry. For
ordinary people, perhaps even for the War Cabinet on their daily commute
to London, the visual evidence of tree felling was more powerful than statistics. A telling account of the cut-and-run felling work came from Della
Gardner, a former office worker who drove a lorry:

We reduced plantation after plantation to a flattened mass of timber [work-
ing our way] through the Chiltern Hills, Ibstone, Turville, Fingest, Skirmett,
down into the Thames Valley, working in beautiful surroundings from Henley
through Hambleden, Aston, Medmenham and Marlow [exhausting] the
supply of softwood in Buckinghamshire. [And then on to Hertfordshire]
... St Paul's Walden, King's Walden, Breachwood Green, St Ippollitts ...
Fellers from a wide area were concentrated on the village of Codicote, and
thence they felled plantations in Kimpton, Whitwell, Ayot St Lawrence and
Wheathampstead, Weston and Walkern, constantly on the move, swathing
through one plantation and onto the next almost before the trees had hit the
ground.[12]

Russell Meiggs, the wartime Timber Department's Chief Labour Officer, produced, in 1949, the nearest thing we have to an official account of the timber story of the war in his book *Home Timber Production 1939–1945*. He compared the visual perception of tree felling in south-east England with that in north-east Scotland:

> The cutting [was] divided between the countries, but in all it has fallen most heavily on our softwoods. From the top of Richmond Hill, or from Chanctonbury Ring, England still seems a well wooded country. On the banks of the Dee or the Spey clear swept mountainsides suggest that Scotland has been stripped bare. Both impressions are false. The hedgerows lined with trees that pattern the English landscape give from a height a forested appearance which is a delusion. English woods moreover are mostly on the plain and off the main highways; the fellings are not noticeable from the main roads and railways. In Scotland, and particularly in the highland zone, the majority of the timber grows on the mountain sides and a clear-fell is inescapable to the eye.[13]

At the end of the war the case for forestry in Britain must have seemed irrefutable. Altogether, 46 per cent of the nation's stock of growing timber was cut down for the war effort. And if there had been doubts about whether home-grown timber would be suitable for the needs of the war period, they were dispelled when it was providing three-quarters of the nation's timber consumption.

Robinson's 'Great Work'

Robinson's war was cut short. He had been appointed as the Deputy Timber Controller with specific responsibility for the production of home timber. But in June 1942, with the tide of the war turning, he returned to London from his office in Bristol to start what has been described as his 'great work' – the planning of post-war forestry. This emerged in June 1943 as the Forestry Commissioners' report on *Post-War Forest Policy*.[14]

We can almost feel Robinson's sense of frustration. Twenty years of single-minded commitment to the task of rebuilding Britain's timber resource had produced some impressive physical results on the ground, but had not produced the timber when it was needed; the new forests were simply too young to contribute to the war effort. As he put it in his policy report:

the forestry position is much worse than in 1918 and a re-orientation of thought is necessary. Our woods and forests must be made adequate for our national requirements, and to that end they must be increased in area, replanted where necessary, conserved, developed and utilised. The whole, and not merely tree planting, must be the goal of future forest policy.

What of *private* estate forestry in this great leap of ambition? Robinson was well aware of its neglected state and had been on the receiving end of much lobbying about it. The Forestry Act of 1919 had made provision for grants and loans for private landowners, but a desire to get results quickly through state forestry had frustrated that particular aim in the Acland report. When another great patchwork of war-devastated woodlands was threatened, adding to the backlog from the First World War, Robinson could only anticipate further neglect and loss of land to agriculture. Plainly, he thought, only the force of law would persuade landowners to replant their felled areas. What financial incentive, he wondered, would be needed to sweeten the pill?

The effect of farming policy also had to be considered. Farming, not forestry, was the sitting tenant in most of the countryside, and farmers had again (as in the First World War) been on the receiving end of a huge political push for food production. Would that political interest continue after the war? Farmers speculated that it would not. But the likelihood that Britain could obtain its food needs from abroad after the war seemed remote, and already by 1943 a political turnaround on agriculture was in the wind. Buoyant periods of agriculture had always added to the decline of forests, so any move to provide generous and permanent support for agriculture could have a critical impact on the availability of land for forests.

In 1947, Labour Prime Minister Clement Attlee took the opposite path to that adopted by the Liberal Lloyd George in 1921: he decided on measures to stimulate domestic food production so as to improve self-sufficiency and reduce foreign competition. The Agriculture Act of 1947, followed by other farming Acts in the 1950s and '60s, was designed to encourage a level of stability in the industry that had never been seen before. There would be price supports and 'proper remuneration and living conditions for farmers and workers in agriculture and an adequate return on capital invested in the industry'. The effect was to give agriculture a prior claim to the land over all other uses, a policy that was so restrictive it had to be relaxed a few years later to make way for urban development.

Another straw in the wind for Robinson in 1943 was the expectation that post-war legislation would contain provisions on planning and amenity. The Scott Committee of 1942 had been charged with looking at land use in rural areas and was the inspiration behind both the 1947 Town and Country Planning Act (and the parallel legislation in Scotland) and the 1949 National Parks and Access to the Countryside Act. The roots of the pre-existing planning legislation had grown up in the desire to improve towns, but the 1947 Act extended the planning concept to rural land as well, laying down a framework for the control of building in the countryside. Although forestry and farming were not regarded as development in the ordinary sense (and so were exempted from planning control or, in the jargon, were regarded as 'permitted development'), they were nevertheless increasingly influenced by planning policies in the post-war years.

The 1949 Act brought to a successful conclusion the long campaign for National Parks which had started with Addison and the CPRE, and was championed in the wartime *John Dower Report*. The Act provided the legal framework for National Parks in England and Wales, and created the National Parks Commission. Scotland had a bye on this aspect of the 1949 Act, the concept of National Parks being rejected there through lack of demand and because of opposition from landowners. The parks were to be 'beautiful and relatively wild country in which landscape beauty is strictly preserved; access and facilities for open-air enjoyment are amply provided; wildlife and places of historic interest are suitably protected and established farming use is effectively maintained'. Nothing was said here about trees and woods. The Act also established the Nature Conservancy with a remit that extended across the whole of Britain.

This then was the emerging political background against which the proposals for post-war forestry were developed and put to Parliament in 1943. Forestry was a minnow of government policy compared with the other great matters of the moment, but still packed a punch. The proposals that were passed into law in the Forestry Acts of 1945 and 1947 were, in a way, more of the same. But the change was in the scale and ambition of future afforestation.

Instead of the creation of a three-year emergency wood reserve, which had been Acland's target in 1919, the forestry programme was now pictured not just as an insurance policy against wartime shortages, but as a national investment with 'important peacetime claims on public attention'. Robinson set his sights on achieving a productive forest resource of 5 million acres throughout Great Britain, 3 million of which would be created by afforestation of 'bare' ground. The remaining 2 million was to come from the 'systematic management' of existing woods, mainly through providing assistance to private owners under a new scheme to be known as the Dedication Scheme, described in Chapter 4. He calculated that altogether this would supply about 35 per cent of Britain's normal peacetime timber consumption.

We can detect only a hint of the underlying tensions over land policy in the Robinson report, and these were with agriculture, not with the soon-to-be National Parks or amenity and conservation interests. Food rationing had wearied the nation and it was the vote-winning politics of farming that took priority over everything else. The unspoken reality was that technical advance in agriculture – mechanisation, chemicals and plant breeding – meant that almost all *lowland* sites, if not already improved for agriculture, could readily be brought under the plough.

An important consequence flowed from that conclusion. Afforestation would be confined to the uplands. Farming was never likely to prosper beyond a subsistence level in the upland areas of the country because of the infertile soils and the short growing season 'above the hill dyke'. Robinson, in his policy report, quoted figures to show that the loss of 'rough grazings' to forestry would have very little effect on agricultural production. But he had to choose his words carefully when referring to the replanting of felled woods and the pursuance of forestry in the *lowlands*. The 'weasel words' that satisfied the farming interests in the government were that forestry would be practised in 'those woodlands that are better suited to forestry than for any other national purpose'. To reinforce the message that forestry would not be allowed to go its own way with regard to agriculture, in 1945 the Forestry Commission was brought under the aegis of the government ministers responsible for agriculture in Westminster, Edinburgh and Cardiff, so losing the quasi-independence it had enjoyed since 1919.

'Real Practical Socialism'

Here we leave the ticklish politics of land use and move to the financial implications of Robinson's programme for forestry, which fell not to the Churchill government that had presided over the reconstruction planning, but to Clement Attlee. In 1945, the new Labour government took on the task of adjusting the economy from a war footing to one for peace-time. One of the top appointments in the Labour government was that of Hugh Dalton, a noted outdoors man who was made Chancellor of the Exchequer. His memoirs, *High Tide and After*, have some interesting things to say on forestry:

> As soon as I got to the Treasury ... I at once invited Sir Roy Robinson ... to come to see me. To him I put the question, warning him first that I wanted a sensible and not a wild answer, 'What is the largest sum you could efficiently spend over the next five years on the work of your Commission?' I asked him to come back with an answer in a few days time. He did so. 'Twenty million pounds' he said. 'It's yours,' I answered, 'but I shall want to come sometimes and see how you're spending it' ... I wrote in my diary: 'I have got more sat-isfaction from agreeing to subscribe £20 millions over five years for forestry development than from any other expenditure since I got to the Treasury. This means twice as much in the next five years as was spent by the Forestry Commission in the whole of the twenty years before the war. This is a Socialist investment, in land and young trees, of great long-term value. Real practical Socialism!' And in return for this subscription, Robinson invested me with a Forestry Commission tie, brown and green, for the earth and trees.[15]

Dalton was true to his word about visiting the woods and, more than that, he did so regularly. Particularly (as he recalled), he liked to visit a forest in the course of the weekend prior to each of his four budgets. It seems he formed a warm relationship with Robinson, taking several holidays with him visiting Commission forests and finding him 'a first class com-panion – humorous, frank and full of most varied knowledge'. In August 1946 Dalton and his wife, accompanied by Robinson, spent a fortnight touring in Scotland, including visits to the forests of the Borders which he described as the 'British Black Forest of the future'. In the Cairngorms he urged Robinson:

> to increase his holdings ... as fast as he could and to declare the place a National Forest Park; to provide several Youth Hostels and other simple hotel accommodation and camping and caravan sites near the foot of the moun-tains ... perhaps too to build a shelter, fitted with bunks and blankets, in some inconspicuous place near one of the summits. In such provision we lag far behind many other mountainous countries, in Europe and beyond.[16]

Glenmore was designated as a Forest Park in 1948, and Dalton's prognosis of future demand proved right: by 1955 the visitor facilities of the park were in keen demand and the Cairngorms was enjoying rapid growth as a centre for winter sports.

With a fair wind from government, it was issues of a more practical kind that faced foresters in the late 1940s. Materials and tools of all kinds were in short supply and the bureaucracy of the early post-war years frustrated progress at every turn. Dalton complained about the slow progress on the building of the forest villages at Kielder. Labour was short too. The men and women in the services and in armaments were released only gradually from war duties, and jobs on the land were not greatly sought after. Women, who so recently had returned to domestic life after the end of the war, were now encouraged to return to the land. More forest workers were required for tree planting than could be found in the new rural centres of afforestation, so foresters needed the help of immigrant workers. Polish volunteers, along with others displaced from Eastern Europe, were recruited to help. The long hours and tedious nature of the manual work that was the norm in those years are hard to imagine by the (still tough) standards of today. Public holidays were almost non-existent and even Christmas Day was a working day in some parts of Scotland,[17] many Scots preferring to postpone their few festive days until New Year.

The creation of large new forests in the hills meant not only the planting of trees, but also the settlement of large numbers of people in and around the forest. Housing was therefore a key part of the Robinson plan because, following the interwar recession in agriculture, there was no modern housing to be found in rural areas. The watchword was improvisation. Factory-built prefabricated houses were hastily put up. Temporary houses were constructed from ex-army barracks salvaged by demolition contractors and resurrected as small two- and three-bedroom houses. Given a lining of plasterboard and an outer cladding of pebble-dash on wire mesh, the houses were said to be warm and comfortable.[18] Meanwhile, 'bothies' were used for itinerant workers. They were not, however, the bare and remote stone-built mountain retreats of popular conception, but more often a 'recycling' of the camps that had been built for the unemployed in the 1920s and '30s.

John Keenleyside, at one time a research worker with the Forestry Commission, remembered the deprivations of the so-called Dublin Bothy in Ardross, Easter Ross, which was said to have got its name from the Irish labourers that built Ardross Castle in the 1880s.[19] It was a large wooden hut with a corrugated iron roof that noisily expanded and contracted with every change of temperature. The rough-sawn boards that made up the walls were 'creosoted liberally every year to preserve the wood and ensure that in the event of fire it would burn well!' The building comprised a dining room, a dormitory with thirty-two narrow ex-army beds and a small kitchen where the cook toiled to make Sunday's brew-up of broth last for the next six days. The 'inmates' were a mix of semi-permanent forest workers and itinerant employees such as ploughmen, mechanics and the 'sample plot' party which went from forest to forest measuring the growth of trees. Bothies like this were brought into service all over Scotland and the north of England: Glen Affric, Fort Augustus, Glenbranter, Kielder, Hamsterley and the North York Moors all had their bothy accommodation. Their working life was, however, a short one; they were summarily closed down in the late 1950s.

Forest villages were intended as the permanent solution to the problem of rural housing and new ones had to be built. The Commission had been pleased with their pre-war venture into smallholdings, and by 1943 they numbered 1,500. Smallholdings, however, took up too much land and there was a need for full-time employees, not part-timers. The potential advantages of villages were clear. Each village would settle a substantial core of forest workers and their families. Not only would they be on the spot for the men's daily work, but the householders could keep an eye on the forest and its security and be available outside the normal working hours for such things as fire duty.

Moreover, by concentrating people in the setting of a village, the Commission hoped to provide village amenities, like a shop, Post Office, pub, school, playing fields and even a village hall that could be used as a church or chapel. The village of Dalavich on Lochaweside, built between 1950 and 1955, comprised forty-seven houses, a new school, a Post Office and a community centre. The population in the Inverliever area was just fifty-five people when the Office of Woods had first acquired land there in 1908 (see Chapter 2), but by 1955 it had swelled to 318 people, while the school roll had increased from 11 children to 127.[20]

Marjory Scott, in her book *Reflections, Recollections*, remembered her days at the village school that served the new settlement at Achnamara, near Lochgilphead in Argyllshire:

At first there was only a trickle. They arrived as each house was completed. Their fathers, some from the slums, but all from Glasgow, had been given these houses, complete with gardens, to rent from the Forestry Commission on condition that they worked for that body just as most of our fathers did. This must have been like paradise for them, for to us locals they seemed a motley crew ... No one minded however, as desks which had long stood empty gradually became occupied. Now, for the first time that even our parents could remember, the classroom was filled to capacity. The desks ... touched one another nose to tail and were regimented into parallel rows ... The classes were arranged across the rows in order of seniority from the back. I came about the middle.[21]

The choice of 'greenfield' sites for many of the forest villages was often controversial. There could be real isolation in a village that housed families all of whom were dependent on a single employer, and where the distance to the nearest market town discouraged social interchange with the outside world. The housing plan for Kielder Forest, for instance, comprised 250 houses centred mainly in a complex of three new villages on greenfield sites. Even as the houses were being built doubts began to creep in. Should the villages have been sited closer to existing settlements? When the North Tyne Railway linking Hexham in England with the Scottish border town of Hawick was closed in 1956, it dealt an unexpected blow to the residents there who had so very recently moved in; no joined-up government policy here! One Kielder villager who went to a football match in Newcastle, 'left by bus at 6.30 am ... and returned at 12.30 am'.[22]

We must digress here for a moment. So long as forestry was dependent on manual methods, there was a need for large numbers of forest workers and for houses for them to live in. But in the 1950s, the mechanisation of forestry began to take off. A number of small engineering firms like Cuthbertson and Parkgate moved into forestry after the war. They developed increasingly large and sophisticated ploughs which could be pulled by a new and more powerful generation of caterpillar tractors, so rapidly taking over the work of ground preparation that had been done before by horse or by hand. The Cuthbertson plough became synonymous with the expansion of forestry in the wet, grass-covered, rolling uplands that were the typical landscapes of the Scottish Borders, Galloway and mid-Wales. In north Yorkshire and the Grampians, where the soils were hard and stony, ploughing was with the RLR and a future generation of more rugged 'tine' ploughs.

The new villages suffered terribly from this development. The introduction of ploughing and the parallel development of harvesting machinery (see

Chapter 8) brought about a big decline in the demand for housing. Kielder village was left unfinished when it became obvious that machines had come to stay. The war had become the turning point in the conversion of forestry to the new mechanical age, and the implications for forestry employment and rural housing ought to have been more obvious. Robinson, in his 1943 policy report, can be accused of some dissembling over his job forecasts, conscious perhaps of the implications for political sentiment about forestry. After the rush of post-war recruitment, the Commission's workforce reached a peak in 1954 of around 15,500 people, and thereafter entered a period of long decline despite the subsequent expansion of planting and harvesting. By 1981 (when the area of the Commission's forests reached a peak, see Chapter 7) its workforce was down to 7,950.

How successful were the forest villages? The answer, it seems, is mixed. The story of forest villages has often been written in pessimistic terms because some of them struggled to develop as communities and the houses lay empty at times. But credit needs to be given to the good homes that many of them provided for people who made a new life on the land. Perhaps the villages are more of a success today than they ever were for their forestry occupants. In the 1970s and '80s, the houses were progressively sold, to be used as homes and weekend retreats for the general population, no longer tied to forestry employment. And rural living today no longer involves the degree of isolation it did sixty years ago. The view that life in the country offers a better alternative to life in the city became fashionable. Today, the Kielder villages, once neglected, are full again. Some people even commute daily by car the 100-mile round trip to Newcastle to work.

Robinson's Legacy

Robinson died in September 1952 aged 69, still in harness as the Commission's Chairman and by then recording an extraordinary thirty-three years at its helm, first as Technical Commissioner and then as Chairman. In 1946 he had been made a peer, becoming Baron Robinson of Kielder Forest in the county of Northumberland and of Adelaide in the Commonwealth of Australia. On his death, his ashes were scattered on the high hills of the Kielder Forest which he had inspired and pioneered from the beginning.

Somehow his lifetime career with the Commission encapsulates the forestry story of his time in a way that no single individual could aspire to or emulate today. To the Commission he was, as George Ryle put it in *Forest Service*, a 'chief who would baulk at nothing to achieve his goal'.[23] To the private forestry sector he was a more ambivalent figure, as we shall see in the next chapter. Leonard Elmhirst, writing in Wilfred Hiley's book *A Forestry Venture*, saw Robinson thus: 'Without [his] twenty-eight years of political bulldozing, Britain might never have achieved a National Forest at all. Parliament had asked him for rapid action against possible future emergencies, and action, not always wise and rarely diplomatic, was taken.'[24]

The year 1953 was the start of a new era. It was also Coronation year. In the Mortimer Forest on the borders of Shropshire and Radnorshire, a bold and confident 'ER' was planted on the hillside using larch and Douglas fir, the former chosen for the letters because of its light deciduous foliage and rapid growth and the latter selected for the darker background (see Picture 20). In South Wales, a commemorative stone marked the naming of the great Morgannwg Forest (now Coed y Cymoedd) and in Scotland the Queen Elizabeth Forest Park in the Trossachs was designated to mark the occasion.

4

WOODS AND PRIVATE LANDOWNERS

W hen, in the seventeenth century, John Evelyn addressed his *Sylva* to 'Gentlemen and Persons of Quality', he did not have in mind 'ordinary Rustics, meer Foresters and Wood-men'. In the book's later editions such people were, however, guided by a glossary of terms so there would be 'no prejudice to the meaner Capacities'. In the medieval era foresters had been responsible for looking after the deer in the royal forests and protecting the trees and undergrowth that provided food and cover for the deer. But by Evelyn's time they were paid employees of the landed estates that were then coming into prominence. Until well into the nineteenth century, foresters were only very lowly functionaries in the hierarchy and economy of the private estates, and the business of tending the woods and forests was a mixture of tradition and slow-changing fashion.

Brief mention was made in Chapter 2 of the 'arboricultural' methods of growing timber that were practised in the nineteenth century. They were epitomised by a well-travelled Scottish forester, James Brown, who, in his 1847 book *The Forester*, pictured the practice as growing trees in 'free air',[1] in other words growing them at wide spacing so that their branches barely touched. We do not have to look far for the historical influences behind this tradition. One was the growing oak for naval timber, usually connected with the practice of coppice-with-standards. The idea was to encourage the lower branches of the standards to grow sideways and so develop into the great spreading boughs that could be used by the shipwrights for 'knees' and 'bends' – the so-called 'compass timbers' that formed the hull of a timber-built ship.

Another influence was the vogue for ornamental planting. Trees planted for ornament and amenity were placed at wide spacing to encourage the broad leafy crowns that looked best in the landscape. Finally, with timber prices falling in the second half of the nineteenth century, the use of woods for shooting was becoming fashionable and pheasants held sway in the woods rather than timber. Well spaced-out trees were liked by landowners; it was the pheasants that paid the bills. Estate foresters were told by their employers to thin out young woods to make way for shrubs and bushes which were planted to provide cover for foxes or pheasants. Rhododendron, azalea, privet and laurel were never so popular.

Infusion of European Ideas

European ideas began to influence the world of forestry in the last two decades of the nineteenth century. Europe led the world in the development of forest science through the influence of German and French foresters' early recognition of the need to conserve forests. In seventeenth-century Germany it was the Thirty Years War and the threat of a wood famine that brought the problem to a head; forests, it was said, were on the verge of ruin. Whereas in France, Jean-Baptiste Colbert, Louis XIV's Chief Minister observed: 'France will perish ... for the lack of timber.'

The principle that evolved from these ancient influences was that of 'sustained yield' or 'sustention'. The idea was that forests should be managed to produce a steady harvest of timber at a biological and economic optimum. That meant that trees were grown close together to make best use of the natural resources of the sun and the soil, and because the natural competition between individual trees would result in better quality timber. To implement this, methods of tree management and regeneration, silvicultural systems, as we know them today, were evolved. After the 1880s, these ideas started to creep into the consciousness of landowners and their foresters in Britain through the advocacy of foresters from Europe and because of the cautious interest shown in them by the forestry journals.

Contrast these European ideas of forest science with the prevailing orthodoxy in Britain of growing trees in 'free air'. The modernisers pictured this orthodoxy as a mixture of obsolete tradition and neglect. The day of the wooden warship was over, and the wood markets of the future, they argued, would want straight, long lengths of timber, free of knots as far as possible, similar to the kind that was imported. What was the point of growing timber for which there was no demand?

Unlikely as it may seem, the staging post for this infusion of ideas into Britain was India. Under the colonial government of Lord Dalhousie, India in the 1850s was the first country outside Europe to adopt a policy of forest conservation. But when it came to the appointment of trained foresters, the absence of any forest teaching in Britain posed a problem for the colonial administrators. Their answer was to send their potential recruits to be trained in the forestry schools of Germany and France and to recruit trained foresters directly from those countries.

The chief propagandist in Britain for the continental approach to forestry was William Schlich (later Professor Sir William Schlich), a German forestry graduate from the University of Giessen. After a distinguished career in the Indian Forest Service, Schlich had settled in Britain with something of a missionary's zeal. In 1885, at the age of 45, he took on the challenge of setting up a forestry course at the Royal Indian Engineering College at Coopers Hill, near Egham in Surrey. The college was run by the India Office to teach engineering and public works to British trainees hoping to make a career in India and Burma. Schlich, however, was not for long satisfied with the limited remit of his college and its training programme. Finding himself right on the spot when the forestry societies' campaigning was gaining momentum (see Chapter 2), he was soon evangelising about the European methods of management well beyond the confines of the college, to landowners and to anyone who would listen. Schlich became a naturalised British subject and in 1889 produced the first volume of his classic work on forestry, the five-volume *Manual of Forestry*.[2]

Confusingly, the textbooks of the time refer to the continental methods by different names: systematic forestry, scientific forestry, systematic economic forestry – take your pick. Forest historians sometimes refer to them as 'new forestry', but Schlich himself deplored this term: 'Some wiseacres have of late been writing about "The New Forestry". Alas it seems to me what is really wanted is to return to "The Old Forestry".'[3] By which, of course, he had in mind the continental science of forestry.

Schlich's precocious ideas were not well received by the independent-minded and cautious landowners in Britain. It is unlikely that the 'full fig' of his European doctrine could or should ever have been applied to the typical landowner in Britain, not least because it required the benefit of a forest area much larger than the small and scattered woodland holdings of most British landowners. Yet there was enough of a silvicultural message to make a difference to those who wished to listen.

All at once, Schlich was accepting commissions to advise landowners all over the country. Not discouraged by long journeys, he travelled as far afield as Ardross in Ross-shire (to the Ardross Estate) and to Devon (the Kitley and Buckland Estate) to produce woodland 'working plans' for estate owners.[4] They were, on the whole, gladly received, but not much acted upon. Authors and publishers of forestry material at the turn of the century tried hard to reflect the 'new' forestry while retaining a patriotic attachment to traditional methods. A.C. Forbes in 1904 in his *English Estate Forestry* was caught between two stools. He felt the need to defend himself for including only one reference to German forestry, but at the same time gave short shrift to the arboricultural methods of the landed estates, which he described as 'a mixture of sylviculture, arboriculture and landscape gardening'.[5]

Plainly, Schlich's 'project' needed reinforcement on many fronts. It needed, for instance, to be linked to a scheme for forestry education and to a programme of properly conducted forest research led by academics open to new ideas – desires, of course, that chimed in every way with the forestry societies' campaigning aims of that time. We have already seen how foresters pressed on a reluctant government the need for forestry education, and how numerous committees and commissions took up the cudgels in support of forestry. Schlich's persistence started to get results at the beginning of the twentieth century. In 1905 the forestry college at Coopers Hill was moved to Oxford, where it evolved into the Commonwealth Forestry Institute.[6] And in the years that followed he was involved in almost every official forestry related committee of those times, including the influential Acland Committee.

Twentieth-century Beginnings

At the beginning of the twentieth century the estate woods were, in some ways, at the height of their arboreal glory. They were good to look at, they were maturing timber investments and they provided the perfect backdrop for their owner's big house and his enjoyment of shooting and sport. The hedgerows and parks were still intact and the excessive tree felling of two world wars was still in the future. But confidence in the future of land-owning was not running high. Overall, the woodland area was declining as financial pressures impinged on estates and the traditional markets for timber were eclipsed by factory methods. This raised important questions about the role that woods could play in the future economy of the estates and explains why the idea of help from the state became popular among landowners. It promised public support for new woods, replacement of ageing ones and a yield of valuable conifer and broadleaved timber which, if grown in the European way, would be of a type and quality that would satisfy the changing timber markets of the time.

Why should the state help to pay for private landowners to plant trees? The Acland Committee saw it as a way of compensating landowners for the outlays they would incur 'carrying out work which is essential to national security, and [which] directly increases the national capital'. Although, they thought, the growing of timber was not in principle different from growing agricultural crops, its subsidisation was justified (where agriculture was not subsidised after the First World War) because the profit derived from the two activities was on completely different timescales. The profit from farming could be obtained within a year or two, while the return from timber growing would occur so far in the future that planting trees could not be regarded as a 'personal investment'.

A Failed Policy

The First World War, it is often said, changed everything. It certainly changed the attitude of many landowners to their estates. The landowners who had survived the war thought that capital invested in farming or forestry was money wasted. When farm tenancies were sold to tenant farmers, the outlying woods were sold off separately. And when farms failed to find buyers due to the agricultural depression that was setting in, the sale of 'surplus assets' was resorted to with landowners selling off their war-felled, but not replanted, woods. Fragmentation of ownership and neglect of woodland was common. Some of the felled woods were bought by the Forestry Commission for the purpose of replanting them, but others were acquired by disinterested property owners such as developers or financial institutions that had come into ownership almost by accident through repossession or death duties.

Even on large and wealthy estates there was a period of hiatus after the First World War. At Chatsworth in Derbyshire, most of the woods that had been felled for timber were not replanted.[7] As the Devonshires reeled from the economic depression, hunting again became the order of the day.

Shooting was often regarded as a frustration for forestry, but, at a time of turmoil in landowning, it was at least an activity that engaged landowners in the preservation of their woods. J.D.U. Ward, a *Country Life* diarist who had little sympathy with sport, recalled in his article:

> In 1927 I worked for a few months on an estate which had about 320 acres of woodlands broken up into blocks ranging from 140 to 5 acres. Here no one ever considered timber seriously: all planting and felling and every other activity was governed first by the needs of pheasants and what would be best for pheasant-shooting, and second by the wishes of the local master of foxhounds. Pheasants and foxes was the estate's proud motto: so long as the woods provided both, and just enough timber for gateposts and minor estate repairs, they were felt to be fulfilling their proper function.[8]

A contributor to the Royal Forestry Society's journal in 1929 thought it was only a matter of time before the million and a half acres of privately owned productive forest would completely disappear, pointing out that only 12,000 acres were being planted by landowners each year, against 20,000 acres that were being felled.[9] The society, in its January 1930 editorial, thought that the problem was one of economics; the landowners' perception was that forestry just didn't pay. The writer urged that a *model* forest be set up as 'a form of social service' to demonstrate how it could be put on a profitable footing.[10]

The English Experiment

Step forward Leonard Elmhirst, who, with economist Wilfred Hiley, emerged as one of the key partnerships in forest history, championing the cause of private forestry when all about them was gloom. Elmhirst, a Yorkshireman, and his wife Dorothy, an American heiress, are best known as the founders of Dartington, the famous experimental school and college near Totnes in Devon which they always referred to as the 'English Experiment'. Their plans for Dartington ranged from education and the arts to the revival of rural industry and the pursuit of forestry and farming. Elmhirst's forestry interest was therefore only a small part of a greater whole. But it increasingly engaged his passion and attention, with the management of his woods and sawmill becoming a hobby as well as a business. In 1926 he was impatient to get going at Dartington and wrote to Lord Lovat for help. 'To your two questions', Lovat is said to have replied, 'how to obtain advice for owners and how to establish a profitable estate sawmill, I can give you plain answers. We are far too busy to be able to spare any of our staff to help and to advise private owners.'

This charmless rebuff, as it was recounted by Elmhirst in later years,[11] was strange. Both he and Lovat shared an interest in bringing to life a depressed and demoralised countryside. But their personalities and backgrounds were very different: Elmhirst was a young go-getting newcomer, full of ideas and not short of cash; Lovat, on the other hand, was the seasoned patrician, already convinced that the days of large-scale landowning were numbered and that only the state could afford the finance needed to make a real difference in forestry. The response clearly rankled Elmhirst, with far-reaching consequences. From the late 1920s he set about promoting the cause of estate forestry within the landowning fraternity and lobbying government officials, arguing that landowners deserved more from the state than they were getting. He thought they should get, in restitution for their wartime losses of timber, advice and practical help, as well as a more generous level of monetary assistance to help them to restore their woods.

Elmhirst, in 1931, acquired a powerful card in his campaign to soften the attitude of the Forestry Commission. The Commission wore two hats, as it still does today; it was responsible for creating and managing the state forests, but also for encouraging private forestry. Elmhirst recruited as his right-hand man Wilfred Hiley, an Oxford don and forest economist, who had just written a classic textbook called *The Economics of Forestry*. As Elmhirst put it, Hiley had quietly walked out of university life to risk his professional future. The relationship between Elmhirst the enthusiast and well-heeled amateur and Hiley the academic was the key to a productive and long partnership, which continued until the death of Hiley in 1961. Hiley produced the bullets for Elmhirst to fire, as well as shooting off some of his own. Together they wanted the private sector to be supported with advice and political help. They visualised 'a future in which the state-owned woods, and all the other woods in the private sector, would produce, in partnership, the pattern of a joint forest economy which might ultimately offer a model for other nations to notice and perhaps to emulate'.[12]

Much of what we take for granted today was new thinking in the mindset of the 1930s. One of Hiley's great crusading themes was the application of business economics to forestry; he could see no point in trying to establish woodlands without taking every economic factor into account and, as Elmhirst said later, 'never stopped asking significant questions about costs, overheads and compound interest'. This was, it seems, a doctrine of little interest to a Commission that, at the time, was concentrating on its political mandate of getting trees in the ground:

> the Commission was laying out a vast forest empire to the best of its ability and as rapidly as possible, and research into the economic problems that the Commission would one day have to face was put deliberately on one side in the interests of the immediate tasks of capital lay-out and development.[13]

If the Royal English Forestry Society (as it was by then known) had vacillated in its enthusiasm for Acland in 1918, it certainly rose to the occasion in the 1930s over help for private forestry, a universally popular cause among its members. Hiley had carefully fostered his contacts among the landowners and, by the late 1930s, along with Elmhirst, had become active in the society. Together they championed the case for private forestry supported by the state and founded on 'proper financial disciplines'. Both the forestry societies had memberships of around 1,600 at this stage of their development, and Robinson found himself at the receiving end of some well-orchestrated lobbying for financial and political support.

By 1938, according to 'the people who knew him' – as Professor Mark Anderson ventures in his monumental *History of Scottish Forestry*[14] – Robinson had mellowed in his single-minded determination to develop state forestry, and was showing more willingness to respond to the calls for help for private forestry. There was talk of a 'Dedication Scheme': a scheme of financial support based on a legally-binding agreement between the state and an individual forest owner. This was a completely novel concept for which Elmhirst and Hiley subsequently claimed much of the credit.[15] An owner joining the scheme would commit himself to manage his woods in perpetuity in exchange for financial help from the public purse. This would mean making his woods productive and managing them in accordance with an agreed 'plan of operations'. The idea was floated in Robinson's policy report in 1943. His hope was that 2 million acres of productive forestry would come from the 'systematic management' of existing woods, mainly through providing assistance to private owners under the new scheme.

Were the government and the Commissioners right about private forestry all along? Robinson was on the defensive arguing that the social, economic and political environments had not been conducive to helping private forestry. He probably had a point; with the Board of Commissioners still dominated by landowners at that time, they ought to have got it right.

Now, however, times were changing. The Second World War was inflicting another round of savage cuts on woodland. So ferocious was the tree felling in the south of England that the War Office demanded a complete stop to it because of the need for tree cover to hide the build-up of troops and supplies for D-Day.[16] There was no legal requirement to replace the many millions of trees cut down in the two world wars and little motivation among landowners to do so. The possibility that the replanting of war-felled woodland would again be neglected in the aftermath of the Second World War was one that was too awful to contemplate. Would the Dedication Scheme be the answer?

After the Second World War: Dedication and Duty

The Dedication Scheme eventually passed into law in the Forestry Act of 1947, but was not implemented until 1950 when details were agreed with landowners' organisations. It seems that Elmhirst, Hiley and the group of forestry society enthusiasts who had led the crusade for the scheme had no mean task selling the concept to their memberships. Was it the back door to nationalisation, landowners wondered. It was not, of course, the idea of financial help that concerned them but the prospect of committing themselves to a legal obligation to practise forestry in perpetuity. Their concerns were to be expected – landowners' suspicions of new ideas ran deep. In 1950, the presidents of the two societies finally advised their members 'who own land which is suitable' to proceed.[17] The Commission mounted a roadshow to publicise the scheme among landowners and agents. Two hundred people attended the event at Llandovery in September 1950, keen to hear what was on offer. It was a tough meeting with the suspicion, in the background, that it was a prelude to nationalisation. The landowners, according to one observer, were offered a stark alternative, being 'officially invited to put their woods in order or alternatively to lease or sell the land to the Commission'.[18] It was persuasion enough; the scheme quickly caught on.

Most likely, the threat of the nationalisation of forests was real enough. It was a new situation and, as Robinson had said, much worse than in 1918. At a time when the Labour government of 1945 was nationalising the strategic industries like the railways and coal, it would be surprising if it had not considered taking control of the timber supply. John Gaze, a former National Trust Land Agent, confirms the point in his book *Figures in a Landscape – A History of the National Trust*. The Trust was 'defensive and suspicious' of the post-war Labour government's policy of nationalisation, and it was only with 'extreme reluctance' that it agreed to consider dedicating its woods.[19]

Moreover, the Trust was reluctant to dedicate its woods for another reason. How was its commitment to conservation to be reconciled with the main aim of Dedication – the production of timber? It was, Gaze tells us, through the influence of George Ryle that the National Trust's doubts were overcome. Gaze offers that Ryle 'was a wise and sensitive man, flexible in his approach to problems and free from the prejudices which too often accompany professional expertise'. Ryle produced a working plan for the Trust's Box Hill Estate in Surrey, which showed how 'amenities and forest management for full timber production are completely compatible'. What seems to have softened the resistance of the Trust was the view that 'English forestry had advanced a lot and had become less dependent on European patterns on which it had been modelled earlier'.

Profitable Forestry?

The manner in which landowners rallied to Dedication was, in the end, overwhelming. The scheme (along with a complementary plan for smaller woods known as 'Approved Woodlands') engaged the interest of half the woodland owners in England and Wales, and nearly *all* of them in Scotland.[20] Chatsworth in Derbyshire dedicated 3,200 acres[21] and Buccleuch, with estates in both Scotland and England, was said to have put 18,000 acres into the scheme.[22] Of course, the financial benefits were a big incentive to join. Money helped landowners to employ a forester and a permanent squad of forestry workers.

If the legal niceties of Dedication had been a reason to hesitate at the beginning, the practicalities of drawing up woodland working plans and implementing them were more of a pleasure. There was much to be done. Lord Bolton in Yorkshire was another enthusiast for Dedication, and a vigorous exponent of forestry:

At the present time, and for many years past, the proportion of poor-quality timber produced in our woodlands has been distressingly high. There is no reason why this should be so; we have some of the finest soils in the world and our climate is ideal for the growth of a wide range of valuable timber trees. This is true of the greater part of the country and a steadily increasing number of owners are taking advantage of the fact and, by the practice of good forestry, are building up a store of first-class timber which is already of great value to themselves and will be still more so to their successors.[23]

Another rallying cry in the 1960s was the late Cyril Hart's *Practical Forestry for the Agent and Surveyor*, a weighty tome of over 400 pages in which he urged land agents and factors to brush up their forestry skills. A land agent himself and a verderer of the Forest of Dean, his view on the attitude of landowners seemed almost to hark back to an earlier age. 'Woodland management', he said, is 'much in favour among private landowners. Such reasons include social tradition, the wish to benefit one's heirs as one's ancestors made similar provision, and the fact that woodlands, always developing and often regenerating themselves, provide in their trees wealth to be tapped when needed for capital improvements, estate duty and other charges.'[24]

When it came to the practical aspects of Hart's book, several pages were devoted to the dos and don'ts of 'thinning' a wood – an activity that seems to have held a particular fascination for some of the high-profile landowners. The purpose of thinning is to give more growing space to well-shaped and vigorous individual trees, and to remove the poorer ones, hopefully for a profit. Thinning can make or mar a plantation in both its composition and in its financial return. Elmhirst, as his secretary Gladys Burr recalled, 'had a little rest after lunch and then he would say, "I am off to the woods". I could see him through my window with three large axes over his shoulder and his yellow helmet.'[25] The 8th Duke of Buccleuch (a one-time President of the Royal Scottish Forestry Society) was another who is said to have enjoyed the challenge of selecting trees for thinning in his 'policy' woods. A then (1950s) junior estate forester at Drumlandrig in Dumfriesshire recalled that the duke gave so much time to the consideration of each and every individual tree that no physical tree marking was ever necessary, his staff simply remembered which trees were to be saved and which cut down![26] The duke's woods were widely regarded as a model of good silviculture. Elmhirst tells the story of how Lord Robinson had once:

begged the Duke to entertain the Minister of Agriculture and himself in order that the Minister might see a whole woodland area still in private hands, expertly planted, cultivated and harvested, perhaps as efficient a total operation on a large scale as any that could be seen at that time in the whole of Britain.[27]

Timber vs Scenery

A prominent feature of Hart's book and several others of its time was advice on what trees to grow where. Guidance, for instance, was given in Mark Anderson's *Selection of Tree Species*, a handbook and ecological guide to the choice of trees for particular kinds of sites. By the 1980s, however, a new dimension had been added to the various influences affecting the choice of tree species, one that had been hardly mentioned in the silvicultural cook books of the 1960s. Roger Parker-Jervis, the agent at the Hampden Estate in the Chilterns, put his finger on it in 1982 when commenting on the predicament of private owners who 'wholeheartedly desire to sustain the traditional country scenery', but who felt that efficient estate management demanded otherwise:

> The need for any owner to convert mainly to a softwood rotation when a mature stand of hardwood has been cleared is overwhelming. The inescapable conclusion must be that it simply cannot be justified as sound estate management to grow broadleaves on anything like the 150 year rotation which, given existing tree species, climate and soil conditions, is currently common practice.[28]

So it was that a major conflict of ideas came to the surface. Were woods to be used for timber production alone or were they to be a landscape feature? Could the two be combined? Even as Parker-Jervis was making these observations, the substitution of conifers for broadleaves was becoming a controversial aspect of forestry practice, noticed beyond the world of foresters alone for its impact on the landscape, and especially so by an emerging environmental movement urging the preservation of traditional landscapes. Where in the drive to improve the productivity of woodland and to modernise forestry did the views of the wider community come into play? If the grants paid to landowners meant anything at all, where was the balance between timber for the landowner and amenity for the wider public? And,

buried deep in the dilemma posed by Parker-Jervis, was the emerging interest in 'ancient woods'.

Ancient Woods

It is not often, in the generally rather placid world of woodland affairs,
that a completely new issue comes to the fore with the same speed and
intensity as the 'discovery' of ancient woods. Ancient woods, as we now
know them, are woods that have been in continuous existence since the
year 1600 (1750 in Scotland) and may even retain some of the ecological
features of the original wildwood. The popular interest in them can be
traced back to the publication of Dr Oliver Rackham's acclaimed book
Trees and Woodland in the British Landscape in 1976[29] and its revised second
edition, first published in 1990.[30] Rackham presented a new way of thinking about old woods, highlighting how they help people to understand
the evolution of the landscape and pointing to their historical value, not
just as ecological reserves but as relics of ancient 'woodmanship'. That they
came to prominence when they did was for two reasons. First, it reflected
a new and flourishing public interest in heritage matters in the 1970s,
and second, because there was a real urgency about their conservation.
Rackham contrasted the benign neglect of the hundred-year period to
1945, through which most existing ancient woodland survived, with the
destructive impact of post-war agriculture and forestry practices – the conversion of ancient woodland to conifers and the grubbing-up of woods for
agriculture. The threat to ancient woods, complained conservationists, was
a story repeated in Dedicated woodland, in Forestry Commission forests
and in the management of the many thousands of small woods that make
up the countryside.

In retrospect, the recognition that ancient woods were something special, to be protected and cherished, was slow in coming to the surface.
Conservationists point out, of course, that they knew this all along (true),
but deeper insights than nature conservation alone had been needed to con-
vince foresters and the wider world that here was something to be preserved
at all costs. In the mid-1980s, the collective hand-wringing over the protection of ancient woods got results: a recognition of their special protected
status in forest policy and an embargo on the further loss of woodland for
agriculture. In 1990, Rackham supposed that the era of their maltreatment

had passed into history and that people would try to restore what had been lost; the coming years were to bear this vision out. The legacy, however, remains; the loss of ancient woodland sites will, in the long run, be perceived as the biggest casualty of the drive for timber productivity in the post-war era.

The year 1980 was, in many ways, the high-water mark of traditional estate forestry. Unfortunately for landowners, the comfortable certainty of the Dedication Scheme ended when it was closed to new entrants by the Thatcher government in a political drive for deregulation, and existing schemes were voluntarily phased out.

Success in forestry needs a continuity of purpose over a long period, and Dedication, whatever its shortcomings, had provided this continuity par excellence. The legal covenant on Dedicated woods had largely arrested forest decline and inspired many landowners to restore, replant and manage woodland. After thirty years of existence, the scheme embraced the woods of 5,300 individual landowners in Britain. The 10th Duke of Atholl reflected on it in 1988 with members of the Royal Scottish Forestry Society: 'The Dedication Scheme imposed a real burden on the landowner … and was recorded on countless land titles throughout the country [but] it was a far-sighted and successful scheme in that it formed the base for the great expansion of private forestry which has taken place since the war.'[31]

After Dedication

Plainly, Dedication was seen as outdated. What would be put in its place? And where were the benefits that would justify continued public support for woods? In the early 1980s public expenditure was squeezed and the still-to-come forestry tax changes would be a further blow to some landowners' ability to maintain productive woodland. Forestry grants after Dedication were of short-term duration (so it proved) and increasingly came with strings attached, such as requiring owners to provide recreational access or tangible environmental 'add-ons'. What effort, landowners wondered, should be put into timber production in the face of mixed signals from the government and uncertain opportunities for funding? That remains a big question today.

In the 1970s and '80s, two new forces in landownership emerged to take over the limelight from the private estates. One was the evolution of company afforestation, a development that is covered in the next chapter. The other was the increasing ownership of woodland by voluntary bodies, sometimes known as the third sector. Neither strictly private nor public, the voluntary bodies and community groups enjoyed a period of great public support at the end of the nineteenth century that chimed well with the green objectives of governments, and continues to do so today. By 2003 the extent of their combined woodland ownership was approaching 100,000 hectares,[32] a trend that will be explored further in Chapter 9.

5

AFFORESTATION: LAND AND LANDSCAPE

Any forest historian is bound to pause over the few years at the end of the 1950s and the early 1960s when events combined to give a real shape and purpose to the afforestation programme, which had been only vaguely sketched out by Robinson in 1943.

Zuckerman's 1957 report on marginal land[1] is a good starting point for this chapter for its insights into contemporary thinking about upland land use. Rural reconstruction was the topical concern of the government in the 1950s and the key question was whether Britain could be made self-supporting in food.

Zuckerman and his committee explored the scope for increasing food production from marginal land and arresting population decline in rural areas. The big problem of the hill farms was the harsh climate and 'a progressive deterioration in the fertility of the soil'. Yet he saw the profitable use of such land as 'vital to our national well-being', if not for farming then for forestry. 'We cannot view with equanimity the under-use, amounting in places to abandonment, of much marginal land made up of rough grazings and waste lands. These categories of land, extending over 20 million acres, constitute almost two-fifths of our land surface.' And while, in the aftermath of the two world wars, no one had doubted the *strategic* reason for growing timber, Zuckerman and his committee thought that there was no prospect of another siege war in the new age of the atomic bomb. The forestry programme, he thought, should have a recognised social and economic purpose.

It was only to be expected that a government-inspired programme of afforestation would have a social purpose: almost from the beginning of the twentieth century forestry had been seen as a way of halting the population decline in remote areas. But there was more than a hint in Zuckerman of the need for a more commercial approach as well, and, of course, they were in some ways contradictory aims. The concentration of forestry in outlying and disadvantaged areas of the country would not produce the most timber or the best financial outcomes. And it was the commercial aim that got the upper hand in forest policy. When the Forestry Commission reflected on the outlook in its 1959 annual report, it said: 'The problems of creating and establishing the country's forest estate have largely been solved; the problems of how to manage it so as to reap a return on the investment, while at the same time preserving the asset so laboriously built up, are now to be faced.'

The stirrings of commercialism were also felt in the private sector in the 1950s and '60s with the development of large private forestry companies. It had never been thought likely that business interests with no previous connection with the land would contemplate an activity with such a long investment cycle. Neither Zuckerman nor Robinson before him had foreseen the development of the companies that would play a part in the task of afforestation that had hitherto been the main preserve of the Forestry Commission.

The National Parks Experience

It seems obvious today that the post-war National Parks and Forestry Acts were destined to collide. The ten National Parks designated under the National Parks and Access to the Countryside Act, 1949 (seven of them in England and three in Wales) came into being between 1951 and 1957. If there were any guesses as to where a clash of interests might occur, they would not have included Exmoor, the second smallest of the parks and far away from the pre-war dispute over afforestation in the Lake District. But Exmoor National Park, almost from the beginning in 1954, had a struggle to assert itself. A series of land use rows – first about afforestation, and later about the 'reclamation' of land for agriculture – were never far from the surface in the early days of the park.

In 1957, one of the principal landowners on Exmoor, the 4th Lord Fortescue, approached the Forestry Commission to offer them a lease of 1,200 acres on the Chains, a high-lying tract of blanket bog which was the gathering ground of the main Exmoor rivers and the wildest and least productive part of the moor. His lordship's worthy but probably misguided objective was to mitigate the threat of a repeat of the Lynmouth Flood Disaster through the beneficial effects of tree planting. Lynmouth, a small coastal village on the northern fringe of the moor, had been the victim of a catastrophic flood on 15 August 1952, when the rivers East Lyn and West Lyn burst their banks. The source of the flood was heavy and prolonged rain, capped by a cloudburst over the Chains. Lives were lost and the village substantially destroyed.

Forests help to regulate stream flow and flooding because the large amount of plant material in the forest and its soils act as a kind of reservoir by intercepting and holding back rainfall, then releasing it slowly. For this reason, water catchments are often planted with trees. It seems unlikely, however, that the afforestation of an ancient bog would have improved matters; it is more likely that it would have increased the risk of flash flooding through the drainage system needed for tree planting. Good or bad, the hydrological objective was soon lost from sight in a row about the aesthetics of afforestation in the National Park. The proposal sparked off immediate opposition from admirers of the park who saw it as a threat to the beauty of the open heartland of Exmoor. It was, as the Chairman of the Exmoor National Park Committee observed, 'a delicate matter' that exposed the tensions between scenic conservation and economic development. 'On the one hand the natural beauty of the park must be preserved, while on the other, the local livelihood of the area must continue.'[2]

It was not an argument that the Forestry Commission had an appetite for after its setback in the pre-war Lake District. When, in June 1958, the Lords Radnor and Strang – the respective chairmen of the Forestry Commission and the National Parks Commission – met and walked the ground, Radnor agreed to withdraw from the proposal.[3] But talk of afforestation rumbled on and press speculation was that 'forestry syndicates' were intent on acquiring land on Exmoor, Dartmoor and Bodmin Moor. The feared afforestation never happened but the doubts remained, inspiring the creation of the Exmoor Society and similar societies on the nearby Quantocks (an Area of Outstanding National Beauty) and Dartmoor.

It could be said that the whole episode was a local affair which was quickly and sensibly resolved, but of course the implications ran much wider, being lost neither on foresters nor on the wider National Park movement. In 1960, the CPRE (Council for the Protection of Rural England) took up the cudgels, mobilising a national campaign to urge that tree planting on open land be placed under formal planning control, a campaign that it pressed for many years but which successive governments resisted. Instead, in 1961, the government urged the two commissions to work out a voluntary agreement[4] by enlisting co-operation from the private forestry interests represented by the Timber Growers' Organisation (newly formed in 1958 to represent England and Wales) and the Country Landowners' Association.

The 'voluntary scheme for afforestation', as it was called, was a milestone. It was the first attempt to integrate forestry into the planning system and the first bit of serious casework that got foresters round the table with planners to work out a common approach. Drawing its concepts from the 'zoning' of the Lake District twenty-five years earlier, it began with the mapping of landscape 'sensitivities' and an agreement that there would be a complete embargo on afforestation in the most fragile and sensitive heartland of every National Park. Outside the core area, in areas where the landscape was agreed to be of lower sensitivity, restrictions of various kinds were to be imposed, for example limitations relating to the size or design features of forestry proposals. When landowners put forward tree-planting applications for grant aid to the Forestry Commission, the plans would have to fall into line with the criteria and conditions of the scheme.

The implications of the zoning arrangements in Exmoor might never have been tested had it not been for a 'desk exercise' to explore what the scheme might mean in practice. Roger Miles, a landscape architect, forester and rural planner with Somerset County Council, was commissioned by the Exmoor authorities to carry out a study of afforestation prospects in the wake of the Chains affair.[5] Potential sites for afforestation had to satisfy a rigorous set of principles chosen to safeguard the major interests of the park, including those of landscape, recreational use and agriculture. The landscape interest was in turn expressed in terms of the size and shape of a wood and how it would fit in with its surroundings and satisfy recognised principles of good design. Having taken account of the various constraints, the survey produced the result that 4,000 acres, representing about 2.5 per cent of the park area, might be afforested; an area that would increase the tree cover in the park from 10 per cent to 12.5 per cent. This, however, was in individual sites of under 100 acres each. It seems unlikely that in the realpolitik of the National Park committees this lean outcome for forestry would have become a reality, and in later years few of the chosen sites were ever planted. Foresters saw the opportunities as too limiting and increasingly turned their attentions elsewhere.

1. The Ewehurst Park sawmill, Hampshire, in 1909. Steam engines provided the motive power for this typical estate mill and horses were the 'careful movers'. The mill foreman (second left) was a Scot, Alex Paterson, from Falkirk. ©*The Trustees of the National Museums of Scotland*

2. Timber harvesting on the Ewehurst Park Estate. The oak trees in this harvesting scene have been stripped of their bark for tanning. ©*The Trustees of the National Museums of Scotland*

3. Sandwich break. In the First World War the Land Army women working in forestry were formed into a separate unit known as the Women's Forestry Service. © *Hulton Archive/ Getty Images*

Above: 4. Leaves on the line? A group of forest workers pose by a great beech log on a railway wagon in the High Wycombe area in 1917. The temporary railway lines enabled a horse to pull much greater loads of timber to a sawmill or railway company siding. © *High Wycombe Library*

Left: 5. Lord Lovat, 1871–1933. The widespread felling of woods in the First World War led to the formation of the Forestry Commission in 1919; Lovat was its first chairman. *From F.O. Lindley (1935) Lord Lovat: 1871–1933, Hutchinson and Co.*

6. Roy Robinson, a 'chief who would baulk at nothing to achieve his goal'. Here photographed around 1950, he was appointed as the Forestry Commission's first Technical Commissioner in 1919 and served as its Chairman between 1932 and 1952. © *Royal Forestry Society*

7. From Belize at the end of the mahogany season to a wintry forestry camp near Duns in Berwickshire. Honduran lumberjacks felling and extracting timber with Australian engineers in the Second World War. © *Hulton Archive/Getty Images*

Left: 8. Making light work of it. A forestry camp in Surrey in September 1940. In the Second World War the timber authorities had a scheme for the employment of schoolboys during the holidays. There were thirty-eight such 'school camps' in England and Wales. © *Hulton Archive/Getty Images*

Below: 9. The supply of pit props was critical to the war effort. It is difficult to find illustrations of coal miners working underground because of the risk posed by exploding flashbulbs. This picture (from an unknown colliery) was taken in 1941. © *Hulton Archive/Getty Images*

10. They also served. A sculpture erected at David Marshall Lodge in Perthshire in 2008 as a memorial to the part played by the lumberjills in the two world wars. © *Forestry Commission*

11. Gloucestershire, October 1945. Many hand crafts were revived in the Second World War when manufactured goods were hard to obtain. Here pipes are being made from cherry wood for sale at a roadside stall. © *Hulton Archive/Getty Images*

12. In the Nagshead Plantation, Forest of Dean, 1955. In the nineteenth century every leather worker was dependent on tanbark stripped from trees. By the 1960s, the trade had died out. © *Forestry Commission*

13. Working woods and working horses, at Fingest, Buckinghamshire in 1955. The characteristic beech woods of the Chilterns were planted in the nineteenth century to serve a burgeoning furniture industry. © *Bucks Free Press*

14. Pit-sawing like this was the old way of cutting timber before sawmilling became commonplace in the nineteenth century. Remarkably, here is the practice still in use in Torling, Essex, in 1966, where the blacksmith and his assistant are sawing up a small oak tree. © *Hulton Archive/Getty Images*

15. Working in the gloaming. Modern tree-harvesters are highly productive and, with their powerful lights, can work through the winter months and in the twilight. The introduction of harvesters in the 1980s did away with back pain and other complaints associated with the full-time use of a chainsaw. © *Forestry Commission*

16. Giddings sawmill in the New Forest, pictured in 2007. In contrast to the labour-intensive estate sawmilling of the early twentieth century, illustrated in Picture 1, the modern mill is highly mechanised and controlled by just one man and a computer. © *Forestry Commission*

17. Not a pretty sight. The cultivators of this unsightly rectangular experiment on a windswept Welsh mountain thought nothing of its visual effect when it was planted in 1929. The plots on the northerly slope of Cwm Du at Beddgelert were an experiment to test the suitability of different kinds of trees for growing at high elevations. The trees were felled in the 1980s. © *Forestry Commission*

18. Blackhall Spinney, Sevenoaks, in 1958. The seed collected from these fine 200-year-old beech trees was distributed throughout Britain for growing in forest nurseries. © *Hulton Archive/Getty Images*

Left: 19. Forestry houses in the village of Ford at the head of Loch Awe in Argyllshire, built in the 1950s to serve the burgeoning expansion of forestry. The extreme remoteness of many of the clusters of houses and small villages is well illustrated in this picture. © *Falkirk museums. Licensor www.scan.ac.uk*

Left: 20. Kinsley Wood, Radnorshire in 1965. The trees were planted in 1953 to celebrate the coronation of Queen Elizabeth II. The road in the foreground is the A488 from Shrewsbury to Knighton. © *Press Association*

Below: 21. The M5 in Gloucestershire in 1978. Tree planting on the cuttings and embankments of the motorway network in the 1960s and '70s converted a barren engineered landscape into a tolerably restful driving experience. © *Forestry Commission*

22. A farmed landscape in the Tweed Valley in the Scottish Borders. Contrast the rather curious pattern of twentieth-century woodlots and shelter belts in the background with the nineteenth-century landscape of traditional squarish fields in the foreground. © *Forestry Commission*

23. Tree planting in water catchments was very much the thing to do in Victorian times. Nowadays over half a million people a year visit Tarn Hows, a noted beauty spot in the Lake District designated as a Site of Special Scientific Interest in 1965. The pines, larches and spruces were planted in the 1860s. *Author's Collection*

24. Loch Katrine in the Trossachs. Following suspected cryptosporidium pollution in Glasgow's water supply in the 1990s, sheep farming in the catchment was ended. The surrounds of the loch are now the centrepiece of a 21,000-hectare conservation project to restore woodland and encourage wildlife. © *Forestry Commission*

25. Kielder Forest in Northumberland in 2005. The first stage of 'restructuring' in which large even-aged expanses of trees are broken up into more aesthetically pleasing management units. © *Forestry Commission*

26. Urban regeneration: tree planting in 2006 at a former landfill site at Moston Vale in the Red Rose Community Forest near Manchester. © *Forestry Commission*

27. A shooting scene on an Oxfordshire estate in 1910. Gamekeeping took precedence over forestry in the Edwardian era, during which Britain became almost wholly reliant on imported timber. © *Hulton Archive/Getty Images*

Left: 28. Woodland has always been attractive to picnickers, but this party were fortunate to find a wood still standing in the immediate aftermath of the First World War. © *Hulton Archive/Getty Images*

Below: 29. Caldon's Farm campsite at Glentrool, pictured in the 1970s. The Glentrool Forest Park in Galloway was established in the 1950s. © *Forestry Commission*

30. Planning success! In March 1999, Friends of Penn Wood in the Chilterns and other campaigners met to celebrate their success in winning a court battle against the construction of a golf course in the wood. The wood was saved through the fund-raising efforts of the local community and the Woodland Trust. © *Bucks Free Press*

31. December 2006 in the New Forest, Hampshire. Local residents, naturalists and foresters meet to discuss the management of one of the enclosures. © *Forestry Commission*

32. An 'all-ability' access track in mixed woodland in the Forest of Dean, Gloucestershire. © *Forestry Commission*

33. Garscadden Wood, Drumchapel, Scotland. In community forestry, problems of vandalism and car-dumping have to be overcome by encouraging community involvement in the protection and management of the woods. © *Forestry Commission*

34. Cathkin Braes, Castlemilk in Glasgow. Urban fringe woodlands provide fine opportunities for recreational use. The Castlemilk estate is an urban part of Glasgow undergoing regeneration.
© *Forestry Commission*

35. In this high-profile visitor facility, people are invited to test their skills and agility on an aerial ropeway at the High Lodge Visitor Centre in Thetford Forest.
© *Forestry Commission*

36. Trees worth meeting. This Douglas fir growing in the Reelig Glen in Inverness-shire is one of the tallest trees in Britain, measuring close to 200ft high. © *Forestry Commission*

37. Husky sled racing – an exhilarating sport that became popular at Kielder in Northumberland and in the Cairngorms in the 1990s. When snow is in short supply, contestants fit wheels to their rigs. © *Forestry Commission*

38. A wildlife hide at Rosliston Forest Centre in the National Forest. Opened in 1994, the centre provides cycle routes, a 'trim trail', archery and outdoor play and craft areas for children. © *Forestry Commission*

39. Kiveton Community Woodland on the site of an old colliery near Sheffield, said to have been one of the world's deepest mines. Here children are sledging on the 'zig-zag' slope. © *Forestry Commission*

40/41. A 'forest school' event near Ruthin, Clwyd, in 2005. Modelled on a Scandinavian concept, forest school teaches children about outdoor living, nature and animals. © *Forestry Commission*

% woodland cover

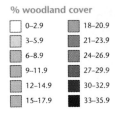

☐	0–2.9	☐	18–20.9
☐	3–5.9	☐	21–23.9
☐	6–8.9	☐	24–26.9
☐	9–11.9	☐	27–29.9
☐	12–14.9	☐	30–32.9
☐	15–17.9	■	33–35.9

1895

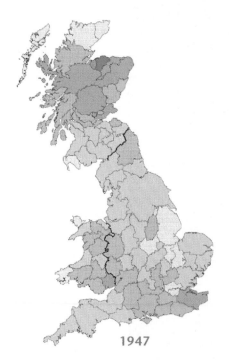

1947

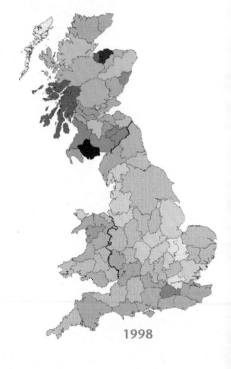

1998

It would be going too far to generalise this outcome to the other National Parks, which all had their own land-use preferences and local politics. Exmoor did not suffer from the fragile upland economy that handicapped most of the northern and western uplands, where a stronger case for afforestation on social grounds could have been made. The larger and more remote parks – Northumberland, the North York Moors and Snowdonia – all had an early history of afforestation and accommodated more. But in general, and with the passage of time, it became obvious that large-scale conifer afforestation was not compatible with the ideals of the National Parks.

Thus the Exmoor precedent had wide-ranging implications for the geography of forest expansion throughout Britain. Along with the AONBs (also designated under the 1949 National Parks Act), the parks *are* the uplands in England and, with their exclusion from afforestation, foresters turned their attention to Scotland and Wales. When the Forestry Commission moved its headquarters to Edinburgh in 1975 (having previously been in London and Basingstoke) it seemed especially symbolic.

Afforestation and Sheep Farming

Hill farming is the epitome of a family affair; it is said that hill farmers are born, not made. Keenly individualistic, each one had his or her story to tell, and his own regret about the passing of a way of life. The very first Forestry Commission annual report predicted that the afforestation of land was bound to cause hardship: 'the cry of mutton versus trees will be raised.' But ill feeling at the transfer of land to forestry was less than might have been expected. A younger generation of farmers was not, it seemed, interested in doing such laborious work for low rewards.

The size of the landholdings offered for sale by hill farmers and bought by forestry interests reflected historical patterns of landownership. An ageing hill farmer in mid-Wales, weary of trying to make ends meet on a modest 50-hectare farm, cashed in on the buoyant forestry land prices as quickly as a shrewd landowner in the south of Scotland who, with a retiring tenant, had a farm of nearer 1,000 hectares to sell.

Decisions to sell to 'the forestry' were personal ones for each farming family but took on the look of a collective force as ownerships and tenancies were given up. Tree planting reflected the places of failing agriculture where short growing seasons and high rainfall contributed to livestock problems and the erosion of nutrients from soils. The favoured spots for planting were upland Wales and the south and west of Scotland, particularly Dumfries and Galloway. Some farms were given up in their entirety, while others got a new lease of life through amalgamation of the better quality 'bottom' land with that of adjoining owners. Thus a kind of land-use pattern emerged from this voluntary process. The valley bottoms were retained for farming, trees were planted on the 'middle ground' and the hilltops – too cold and windy for trees – were left bare for amenity and the summer grazing of livestock.

What about the human side of this development? What were the aspirations of the foresters? George Ryle caught the mood, here referring to the Brechfa Forest near Carmarthen when writing in 1963:

> It was a poor country which the Forestry Commission steadily bought piecemeal from a number of bankrupt large landowners and from innumerable ageing small hill farmers. It is impossible not to look back with pride at this property today. The worst of the old dwellings have been pulled down and are now lost deep in the new forest. The better of them have been modernised and with the more fertile fields have been kept as small holdings for our skilled woodmen. The several little hamlets have been enlarged with new dwellings for woodmen and their families. There is a new school and a new police station. There is a daily bus service where there used to be only one each week. It is today a range of hills and valleys pulsating with life whereas when I first knew it, it was decaying.[6]

The choice of tree species used for upland afforestation has been touched on in earlier chapters. Conifers are well adapted to withstand low temperatures and poor soils, and were capable of a remarkable volume of production in the right conditions. Mention was made in Chapter 1 of the introduction of Sitka spruce to Britain and its importance today as the main commercial tree species; it represents around half of the coniferous area of the country. In contrast to the huge number of different kinds of conifers in parks and gardens, very few species 'made it' as commercial trees in Britain. Either they grew too slowly or they were unsuited to the testing conditions of soils and climate in the upland environment where they were to be planted. As well as Sitka, Norway spruce, European and Hybrid larch (a cross between the European and Japanese species of larch first discovered at Dunkeld in Perthshire), Douglas fir and the Scots and Corsican pines emerged as valuable commercial trees, although the gloss was removed from the latter when, in very recent years, it fell victim to a tree disease.

A much-planted tree that spectacularly failed to live up to its early promise was the Lodgepole pine. Where Sitka was thought of as the tree for mineral soils, the Lodgepole became the tree for the peatlands, mostly grown on the upper fringes of forests where freezing temperatures encourage the development of peat. It was also planted on lowland peat such as in the Flow Country. Perhaps more notice should have been taken of the botanists' chosen Latin name for this variable species: *Pinus contorta*. Thousands of hectares of the now notorious 'south coastal' and 'Lulu Island' varieties were planted before it became obvious that it did not grow straight enough to be suitable for sawmilling. When better provenances of the tree were found (in the inland and more northern parts of the tree's natural range in north-west America), many acres of these poor-growing varieties had to be replaced.

There is plenty in print about the inadequacies of conifers in the landscape, never more forcefully expressed than by Steve Tompkins, an author who could see no merit at all in commercial forestry in his *Forestry in Crisis* which was produced at the height of the Flow Country row. It seems that there is a dichotomy in our attitude to conifers. On the one hand, we may travel thousands of miles to visit the cathedral-like groves of giant redwoods in northern California, or gasp in surprise when a previously undiscovered coniferous tree – the Wollemi pine – is found in a little-known canyon in remote southern Australia, as it was in 1994. On the other hand, admiring a curiosity in a garden or public park is not quite the same as seeing conifers established in large numbers on a previously open and admired piece of countryside.

A variety of impulses come to mind. There is a natural dislike of change and a pleasure in familiarity that can overwhelm almost any rational argument for 'improvement'. In a reflective moment, Sylvia Crowe, the Forestry Commission's first landscape advisor, saw the job of people who plan and work in the landscape as a 'particularly thankless one' because 'There is at present a tendency to oppose change in any landscape without sufficient appreciation of what would be lost and what gained'.[7] And then there is an array of personal experiences, values and prejudices that go to make up the old adage that beauty is in the eye of the beholder. The point to make here is that opinions differ. Tompkins saw afforestation as a 'shattering intrusion' into a semi-natural environment,[8] whereas in 1970 Nan Fairbrother, writing in her *New Lives, New Landscapes*, thought Kielder Forest in Northumberland (one of the more mature forests), 'with its changing patterns of woods and open hills', to be a 'far more varied and interesting landscape'.[9] John Dower, the doyen of the National Park movement, once drew a visual comparison between Kielder Forest and the Lake District:

> The Kielder and Wark Forests will constitute a fine, if sombre, stretch of landscape, providing both timber and employment. The wide scale and easy slopes of the bulk of upland country enables it to take extensive conifer plantations without the artificial and blanketing effects which they so potently and harmfully produce on the steep and delicately varied fellsides of the Lake District.[10]

Another perspective on the new forests was offered by Dr Frank Fraser Darling who, like Dower, hardly needs any introduction in a book about the upland economy. 'How do you get the forests to grow back on long-felled countryside?' he asked in an address in 1974.[11] He was critical of the plantings made in 1919 which he described as 'growing crops of conifers in the German style [which] was about the limit of ambition then', yet saw the Sitka spruce as a necessary stage in the restoration of a permanent woodland economy:

> The Sitka spruce, and the Cuthbertson plough are a godsend whether you like them or not. They enable us to get cover going in which later we can develop true forest. It is the work of a century at least and this span should be accepted by ramblers and similar-minded folk, that the eyesores of which they complain now are the unpleasant stage we have to go through in the re-creation of an ultimate diverse forest which we hope will give pleasure to the eyes of our grandchildren.

That may still prove to be mainly true.

Most foresters today accept that planting practices in the 1960s left much to be desired. Put briefly, the pursuit of the most profitable way of establishing forests did not produce the most sympathetic landscapes. The angular lines of the boundaries of the sheep farms acquired for forestry did not produce well-contoured forest edges, yet economics dictated that every acre should be planted up. Furthermore, afforestation was, almost by its nature, even aged because large areas of land were acquired over a short period of time and the uniformity was accentuated by the use of a single tree species. By the 1960s, foresters knew that something drastic had to be done to improve the image of their work. Preoccupied with the technical and managerial challenges of tree growing, and perhaps dismissing the Lake District dispute of the 1930s as an isolated problem in an area of exceptional sensitivity, the Forestry Commission had been sharply reminded of its responsibilities for the landscape by its experience on Exmoor.

Sylvia Crowe: Some Views are Better than Others

Sylvia Crowe (later Dame Sylvia) was a respected past President of the Institute of Landscape Architects when she was appointed to the Forestry Commission in 1963. Her credentials for the Forestry Commission were perfect. In *Tomorrow's Landscapes*, her first book published in 1956, she had made a plea for more trees in the landscape, believing, as she put it, that its evolution 'cannot stop dead at any one point in history, and indeed in our own lifetime had probably seen the lowest ebb in tree population since the ice age'. Further, she could offer an unemotional and objective eye to the landscaping problems that the critics of afforestation saw in a largely instinctive way, and expressed a point of view that carried weight both inside the profession and in the wider world. She offered the idea that afforestation should be sited where the planted forest would be an attractive and interesting addition to the landscape: 'there may be places where forestry has spoilt good landscapes, but there are many others where it has improved it and still more where forestry is needed, visually as well as economically.'[12]

Crowe's appointment to the Commission pleased her a lot. It was a unique challenge; the canvas of the land the Commission managed was the largest single ownership in Britain. Sometimes she would spend a whole week 'on tour' with foresters looking at everything from the shapes and boundaries of proposed planting areas to the landscaping of forestry houses, and from shelter belts on tenanted farms to picnic sites and car parks. Her task was to persuade foresters to incorporate landscape design principles into their functional way of doing things. Her easy style and light touch made friends and encouraged respect. People warmed to her. There were, it seems, only two hazards to her tours: the damp and the cold. The damp made it impossible for her to do her usual sketches in the forest, and the cold, although she was prepared for it, reduced the attention span of her otherwise attentive students. Crowe had a particular affection for Wales and it was said that it always snowed when she visited Wales. Early in June one year, well prepared for a freeze, she famously sported a squirrel-fur coat – in a smart shade of grey, of course.

The Rapid Expansion of Company Forestry

Another development in the 1960s was the beginning of large-scale affor-estation by private forestry companies, a new phenomenon, quite distinct from the operations of established tree planters like the traditional estate owners and the Forestry Commission. Its investors were wealthy individuals, 'top-rate' taxpayers, who were attracted to an investment idea that was both novel and 'green' – a concept they felt they could identify with. The tradi-tional private landowners, involved as they were in the Dedication Scheme, had, on the whole, neither the money nor the inclination to expand their woodland areas by more than a hundred acres or so.

The particular feature of personal tax that stimulated investment forestry was the notorious 'Schedule D', a perfectly normal tax schedule under which many businesses were taxed, but one, however, that provided an unu-sual opportunity when applied to a business activity with a long-term scale beyond the life of an individual investor. By using this tax option, high earners were able to subsidise their forestry investment by setting off the cost of land purchase and tree planting against the income tax that would have been payable on earnings from their normal occupation.

The idea of turning the tax liabilities of his clients to advantage in the world of forestry is credited to Kenneth Rankin, a chartered accountant in the City of London. His interest in forestry began in the early 1950s when he acquired an interest in a small timber merchant business in the south-east of England. This led him to the idea for a woodland investment scheme. Rankin, however, became frustrated with the lack of a means to put his tax-saving ideas into practice. The woodland management companies that then existed, mostly in the south-east of England, were too small and unambi-tious for him. They drew their clients from the ranks of small woodland owners who had no inclinations beyond their existing boundaries and insufficient incomes to benefit from the favourable tax arrangements. They were also in the wrong place; he soon realised that the big opportunities lay in Scotland and Wales. He went on to form his own forestry management company with the specialist marketing skills needed to attract clients beyond the range of his usual professional services.

So began Rankin's Economic Forestry Group (EFG) in 1959, which actively marketed the idea of woodland investment to wealthy people. It bought the land on their behalf and arranged for the physical work of tree planting and forest establishment to be carried out whilst aiming to make a significant contribution to the national afforestation programme. Offices were opened in Edinburgh and in several towns in southern and central Scotland and Wales. Thus he succeeded in providing both the big idea and the means of realising it. Publicity literature championing the virtues of afforestation as an investment was pitched at wealthy individuals, and seminars were staged to attract investors in London and the Home Counties. His clients came mainly from the worlds of business, media and sport. Meanwhile, political support was garnered through his company's annual luncheon, staged at a prestigious London West End venue, attended by MPs from all sides and enlivened with a speaker from the government of the day.

The actual work of planting trees was, of course, far away from these sparkling city events. In 1965, the EFG acquired the core of what later became its 'flagship' forest of Eskdalemuir in a little-visited backwater of north-east Dumfriesshire. Tanlawhill was the extensive but declining sheep farm that became the nucleus of the mainly forested Eskdalemuir landscape that exists today. The bottom land was retained for agriculture, while the hill pasture was planted with trees. Several adjoining farms were purchased in the years that followed, and the niceties of tree planting and the professional management of a growing deer population there were demonstrated to potential clients and invited guests such as Prince Charles (1982) and a Select Committee of the House of Lords (1985).

The mechanics of company afforestation were straightforward. EFG had a full-time acquisition team that valued the land for purchase and gave the company's clients taxation advice. They sought out hill grazing land that was both easy to plant and situated where a growing forestry presence meant that there would be economies of scale. To avoid antagonism from the farming communities, the company only purchased farms that carried a sheep stocking level of less than one ewe for 1 hectare. When a parcel of land had been acquired, it was matched to their clients, some of whom bought interests in several such acquisitions over a period of time. The larger parcels were split up into a number of interlocking ownership units varying in size between 100 and 500 hectares. The company encouraged its clients to take an interest in their woods by using them for personal recreation or shoot-ing, and also provided limited facilities for public access. EFG grew rapidly, particularly in the south of Scotland. Rankin, together with his managing director John Campbell, built it into the largest private forestry company in Britain which, by 1973, was looking after 70,000 hectares of woodland and employing 800 people. By the 1980s, the Eskdalemuir Forest alone had grown to 22,000 hectares.

Rankin's idea quickly caught on. The 'big four', as they came to be called, were EFG, Tilhill Forestry (which today incorporates the EFG through subsequent mergers), Fountain Forestry (now Fountains, a forest man-agement and investment services company) and the Scottish Woodlands Owners Association (now Scottish Woodlands Ltd). Research in Scotland in 1986 estimated that the big four were involved in 72 per cent of the pri-vate afforestation schemes, while smaller satellite companies and offshoots were responsible for a further 20 per cent.[13] The scale of planting was huge. Where hill farmers had once used binoculars to survey their flocks of sheep on the summer grazings, forestry companies in south Scotland had to use helicopters to map and monitor the early growth of their trees.

In order to succeed as an investment, there needed to be a ready market for any property when its owner wished to sell it. What are collectively known as the City institutions came to the rescue in the 1970s by providing just such a market for the newly planted forests established by the compa-nies and their wealthy clients. Rankin and his competitors pitched the idea of forest ownership to insurance companies and pension funds. At a time of high inflation, the fund managers saw forested land as more inflation-proof than other assets like stocks and shares which were declining in real value. The forestry companies were pleased with the City institutions as purchas-ers because the latter had no interest in the *management* of the forest, which could therefore be retained as a service to be provided by the company. Tompkins estimated that between thirty and forty City institutions entered the forest market between 1975 and 1982, including the Post Office pension fund and those of British Gas and the Midland Bank.[14]

Suitable land for afforestation was getting hard to find when the Thatcher government came to power in 1979. Already the availability of land for pur-chase in Wales had dried up, while in Scotland, intense competition between the big four drove prices up. Under instruction from the new government, the Forestry Commission withdrew from planting, which the forestry com-panies were encouraged to take over with the benefit of the then-existing tax arrangements. The sequence of typical land prices for hill land tells its own story. In the 1950s hill land could be bought for £10 per hectare; by 1970 it was £47 per hectare and by 1980 it was £800 per hectare. Even with the advantage of the tax incentives, it became increasingly difficult for the forestry companies to justify to their clients paying over £800 per hectare for land alone. One solution to the impending land shortage was to turn to the high-lying and remote areas of moorland which had hitherto been thought of as too poor for successful tree growth. Land among the 'high tops' of the mountains above the existing tree line, and land in the peaty lowland areas of Caithness and Sutherland in the north of Scotland, could still be bought for less than £100 per hectare.

The Scottish Serengeti?

And so to the Flow Country: the Flows are a unique area of low-lying flat bogs set in the heart of a great sprawling wilderness of mountain and moorland in Caithness and Sutherland. Few people visited the Flows, hardly anyone lived there and sheep farming had almost been abandoned. It was therefore far away from the thinking of most foresters and conservationists and had not been noted as of particular interest for nature conservation. On the contrary, as we now know, it is outstandingly rich in moorland birdlife: greenshank, golden plovers, dunlins and breeding raptors such as hen harrier and merlin. Its apt name (newly coined in the 1980s) refers to its dark peaty pools that shimmer with reflected light, appearing to 'flow' across the land when the breeze takes them.

Fountain Forestry in the early 1980s was a successful forestry business, looking for expansion but running low on land for planting in what was then its main area of activity in south Scotland. It had over 250 employees and looked after 80,000 hectares of forest. The company had been encouraged by the success of experiments with tree mixtures of Lodgepole pine and Sitka spruce on deep peat. The Lodgepole was what foresters call a 'sacrificial crop'. It was there to suppress the growth of the heather and to dry out the upper layers of peat, so giving the Sitka the opportunity to establish itself in the more amenable site conditions that would then prevail. Meanwhile, ploughs had been developed to drain the peat and provide an elevated and therefore drier planting position for the young trees. The company accordingly decided to open up operations in the far north of

Scotland, including the Flow Country. To Fountain, it must have seemed like the last remaining frontier and a place where there would be few constraints on the planting of trees.

The Flows, in the meantime, has attracted the interest of the RSPB. In 1984, through its house magazine *Birds*, the society gathered the support of its 400,000 members for a public campaign to preserve the bird habitat and resist afforestation. The wetland habitat on which the birds depended would be destroyed by forestry drainage and tree planting would change the open character of the landscape. The society directed its fire at the deeply unpopular Schedule D and at the absentee landowners who were the main clients of Fountain. The society's campaign was headlined by some eye-catching imagery in which the greenshank became its symbol, and the Flow Country was likened to the Plains of the Serengeti[15] – to the astonishment of foresters and many conservationists too. Between 1986 and 1988, the row escalated in an atmosphere of increasing frustration and acrimony, prompting a rash of official reports and new bird surveys which concluded that the Flows contained the richest assortment of upland breeding species in Britain.

The Flow Country was not the first conflict between foresters and conservationists over wildlife. Others had been settled, wisely or otherwise depending on your point of view, by a process of consultation and compromise laid down by the government to resolve disagreements on forest planning. The Flow Country was, however, 'outside the box'. This was because of the rapid incremental development of tree planting and the all-or-nothing nature of the conservation case being made. Both the government's agencies involved, the Forestry Commission (as the main grant-giving body for private forestry) and the NCC (as the statutory nature conservation body), had blundered into a saga which they seemed powerless to control. John Morton Boyd, who retired as the Director of the NCC in Scotland in 1985, described in his book *The Song of the Sandpiper* how his organisation saw it: 'the race was on to acquire land on the one hand for forestry, and on the other hand for conservation.'[16]

One bone of contention was that the challenge to afforestation was orchestrated by a body seemingly far remote from the scene of the action rather than being inspired by local interests. Social and economic factors weighed heavily in the north of Scotland and the expectation of forestry jobs, and the possibility of wood-using industries in the longer run, evoked keen support for Fountain, while the bird interests were accused of frustrating the economic development of the region.

An understanding of the clash between the interests of upland birds and forestry requires a comment on the limitations of the SSSI (Site of Special Scientific Interest) system, a point made by many contemporary conservation writers like Boyd. The SSSI was primarily designed to satisfy a need for protecting wildlife in lowland landscapes when, at a time of rapid agricultural intensification in the 1960s and '70s, the best surviving habitats were restricted to small, well-defined sites. One of its weaknesses, therefore, was that it provided only limited protection for extensive upland areas such as the habitats of moorland birds. If, for example, it was accepted that SSSIs would occupy a representative 10 per cent of a particular kind of habitat, then it was seen as a corollary that there were no nature conservation concerns on the rest. The uplands were, however, almost all semi-natural and could not so easily be divided up between areas worthy of notification as special sites and the remainder. Boyd's opinion on the matter was that the SSSI scheme 'could not be applied' in the case of the Flow Country.[17]

Nor was there any real remedy for the problem in the Wildlife and Countryside Act, 1981. The Act gave the NCC a power of veto over proposed operations that would damage SSSIs, and provided for compensation to be paid to landowners for profits foregone as a result of such a veto. This was the rub. The compensation arrangements were generous to the extent of being counterproductive. Conservationists thought that the financial burden of paying out compensation would discourage the NCC from notifying new sites, particularly very large sites of the kind involved in the Flow Country. They thought too – quite justifiably as it turned out – that valuable sites would be put at risk from proposals that had been 'manufactured' purely to win compensation. In a number of well-publicised cases, this is exactly what happened.

In March 1988 the dispute was effectively brought to an end in a spectacular fashion. Chancellor Nigel Lawson announced in his budget speech that forestry was being taken out of the scope of income tax altogether. This removed at a stroke, subject to some phasing-out arrangements, the main financial incentive that had been the motivation for Fountain and its investors.

The tax change was a big reverse for foresters and its effects went to the very foundations of private forestry. Against this body blow from the government, it now seemed that the formal outcome of the Flows dispute hardly mattered. An 'agreed' report produced by the Highland Regional Council, endorsed by government ministers in 1989, was a middle way that safeguarded the core area of nature conservation interest through the designation of around 350,000 hectares of SSSIs, an area more or less represented by the RSPB's campaign area and the largest assembly of SSSIs in Britain. No 'compensation' arrangements would apply, but forestry would be encouraged in the less environmentally sensitive fringe areas. For Fountain, however, the report's conclusion was academic; the moment had passed and its appetite for land acquisition had gone.

It is ironic that an area almost ignored by both nature conservation and forestry interests until the 1980s has now become, effectively, the largest nature reserve in the country. Although written before the final shots in the battle were fired, the book to read on the subject is Avery and Leslie's *Birds and Forestry*, an especially convincing analysis given the familiarity of the events to both of its authors. The writers were involved directly in the Flow Country through their respective jobs in the RSPB and Forestry Commission. Their conclusion was that the Flow Country is of extraordinary importance for moorland birds and 'one place where it is possible to justify the maintenance of the existing habitat purely on bird conservation grounds regardless of how well the trees might grow'.[18] It could be said that the RSPB was putting its money where its mouth was when, in 1995, it purchased the property at the centre of Fountain's operations, the 7,700-hectare Forsinard Estate. Its purpose was to restore some of the former tree-planted areas to bog conditions, and to show how the peatlands could be developed 'in an environmentally friendly manner with economic benefits for local people'.[19] Few people today, judging by the enthusiasm of the RSPB for its new reserve, would contest the conclusion that it saved a great ecological folly.

After Lawson – Wider Implications

With bird watching a popular hobby on the Conservative government's front bench of the time, perhaps it is true that Treasury ministers had not been too busy to browse the pages of the RSPB's *Birds* magazine? Or, as others suggested, perhaps the clinching shot had nothing to do with either birds or forestry, but the much-criticised forestry tax arrangements. The effect, of course, went far beyond the Flows, to the very foundations of company forestry, and quickly brought an end to the thirty years of large-scale private commercial afforestation inspired by Kenneth Rankin.

There were many implications in the Lawson announcement beyond the immediate concerns of the forestry companies. Lawson, as a kind of quid pro quo, put extra public money into directly paid forestry planting grants. Conservationists favoured this approach because it attracted people whose interest was in tree planting rather than tax saving and was more likely to encourage 'best practice' methods through the grant conditions set by public authorities like the Forestry Commission. The Royal Forestry Society gave a cautious welcome to the changes:

> so that all can see that forestry no longer enjoys an anomalous and apparently highly advantageous position which many envied but few understood, and which all too often lent substance to the attacks of its opponents. We can now argue our case as foresters and not as suspected tax evaders, and that in itself must be worth something.[20]

The Royal Scottish Forestry Society took a more prosaic line, supposing the row over planting to have been exaggerated. The society was 'bemused by the heat of the arguments generated' and pointed out that the physical conditions of extreme exposure and soil meant that 'at least 80 per cent of the land surface [of the Flow Country] could never have a tree rooted in it'.[21]

Planting in the peatlands of remote northern Scotland was one thing, but there were many other situations where tax relief had benefited conservation, and had done so in a way that the more ephemeral directly paid grants for forestry would never do. Tax relief had brought city money into the rural economy in amounts that would never be repeated. Many permanent jobs in British forestry were lost as a result; estates in the 1990s divested themselves of their permanent forestry employees and in-house forester, so weakening their nature conservation activities almost as much as the forestry ones. In 1995 Roger Crofts, then Chief Executive of Scottish National Heritage (the successor body to the NCC in Scotland), described the withdrawal of taxation incentives as a classic example of throwing out the baby with the bath water.[22] Couldn't the Flow Country have been saved more effectively through simple regulatory change? The suspicions remained that the Thatcher government might just have killed off its most effective instrument of forest policy.

Over 1 million hectares were added to the forest resource in the period between 1960 and 1988. The great achievement was the creation of a timber-using industry that was competitive with imports and large enough to look after itself, as Chapter 8 will show. Forestry employment, though it never met the expectations of the forestry pioneers, was still substantial and contributed jobs to the rural economy. The new forests became an important element in the landscape whilst, perhaps enigmatically, Victor Bonham-Carter, author and one-time editor of *Country Life*, described the landscape changes as being 'as bold, in their way, as the concepts that created the enclosure landscapes of the eighteenth century'.[23]

6

THE GREENING OF
FORESTRY

Having considered the planting of 'commercial' forests in Chapter
5, the evolution of their environmental management, particularly
in the state forests, will now be covered. Forestry in the 1960s was
swept up in the vogue for economic planning, and in the public sector there
was pressure to preserve only those services which were self-financing, epitomised by the railways, where Dr Beeching was making his mark. Forests
were no longer seen as a strategic reserve but as a business undertaking in
which productivity and tight cost control became the prime consideration
of many foresters.

The economic philosophy that emerged in the 1960s was not new. Its
first real exposure to practitioners had been in the 1930s when Wilfred
Hiley (see Chapter 4) produced a series of books on woodland management. Before then, forest economics had been a subject for academics rather
than practitioners. Foresters thought that the financial returns from growing timber did not give a fair picture of forestry's many benefits, so the
monetary side was neglected. The lengthy interval between tree planting
and harvesting also posed a problem because it tested the normal principles of business accountancy to its limits. How were investors to compare
the costs and receipts of forest management when tree-planting and felling
operations were separated in time by a period of fifty years or more?

What economists call 'discounted cash flow' methods of analysis are used
to compare expenditures and incomes that are separated in time. The costs
of planting trees and managing forests are translated into financial models
and timber prices are estimated from statistical information over many decades. We need not delve into the pros and cons of this approach to forest

economics because it is the physical outcomes that really count. Costs were reduced and a timber-first philosophy prevailed with little account being taken of the environmental pluses and minuses of tree planting. This meant that anything that reduced or detracted from the economic optimums was viewed as a cost to be avoided or minimised.

How, then, was the gap in forest practice between the timber-related economic optimum and the interests of amenity or the wider environment to be bridged? Consider an example. Sylvia Crowe's work with the Forestry Commission was mentioned in Chapter 5. When she joined the Commission in the 1960s, the pre-war tree plantings from the Lovat era were approaching maturity. Here was an opportunity to remedy ugly planting shapes, introduce more variety and open up new scenic views. It was certain, however, that anything which reduced the volume of wood produced or postponed it to the future was likely to have an economic effect on the 'bottom line' and would therefore be keenly debated. Forest managers were given discretion to depart from the economic optimum to a predetermined limit, say 10 per cent, though this varied according to the sensitivity of the subject under consideration, for example, how conspicuous a landscape viewpoint might be, or whether it was situated in a National Park.

By such means, environmental objectives were gradually assimilated into forest practice, as this chapter will show. To say that it happened in a series of steps (as the headings that follow in this chapter might suggest) would be to give the impression of a planned development, which of course it was not. Rather it was the result of pragmatic change reflecting both technical opportunities and the increasing drift of public opinion towards environmental and social objectives.

The Late 1960s – Forest Recreation

It is hard to believe today – perhaps sitting in a motorway jam on a bank holiday weekend – that the countryside was once seen solely as the workplace of farmers and foresters. Its use and development as a recreational resource unfolded only slowly, and some examples have already been touched on in earlier chapters. By the 1960s, prompted by the mobility that came with car ownership, a surge of recreational interest in the countryside was under way. Town dwellers wanted to get away from their urban environment at week-ends to breathe clean air in green fields, mountains and woods, but people were beginning to put real pressure on 'honey-pot' areas like the National Parks. A series of conferences in the 1960s organised by the Royal Society of Arts and the Nature Conservancy under the banner of 'The Countryside in 1970' brought voluntary bodies, planners and statutory agencies together to discuss how the countryside could be made more accessible to people without spoiling it.

The 1967 Countryside (Scotland) Act and the 1968 Countryside Act (covering England and Wales) were the products of this debate. The Acts, while they gave the two Countryside Commissions responsibility for safeguarding the conservation of the countryside, were intended to encourage its opening up on a broad front – a townsman's charter for the recreational use of the countryside, as some people called it. The Commissions were given powers to encourage the establishment of country parks and to help fund visitor facilities like car parks, picnic places, camping sites and long-distance footpaths for exploring the country.

How did forests fit into this recreational setting? The quiet informal woodland walk had become something of a national pastime in the second half of the nineteenth century, gaining rapidly in popularity with the expansion of the railway system at that time. When, in the 1880s, destinations like Epping Forest and Burnham Beeches were brought into public ownership, they provided what were then exceptional amenities because the woodlands of Britain had been almost entirely in private hands and were mostly inaccessible. The break-up of the nineteenth-century estates in the twentieth century, and the passing of many of them into public or institutional ownership, added a much wider choice of destinations. Arguably, it is this legacy of managed estate woodland that today provides the most popular walking experiences, now more accessible to the public than ever through the National Trust and because of the stately homes and grounds that were opened to the public in and after the 1950s.

At this point we need to introduce the concept of 'multiple use' which surfaced as a planning idea in the 1960s. Multiple use, as the term implies, is where land is used or managed for two or more purposes at the same time. Forests in the United States are sometimes regarded as the supreme examples of resource usage because they serve many interests and provide a model for the integration of economic and non-economic uses of land. Thus, timber, recreation, wildlife and watershed protection are all treated on an equal footing. The idea of multiple use in the publicly owned national forests of that country was a well established one but, until the 1960s, lacked the force of law and had become contentious because of competing pressures. Logging interests, for example, wanted to expand the harvesting of trees when timber supplies became scarce in the private- and company-owned forests that the industry had traditionally exploited. At the same time, there were strident calls from wilderness and amenity societies for preserving tracts of forest as untouched wild areas, so as to remove them from the unwanted attentions of the loggers.

The Multiple Use Sustained Yield Act of 1960 established the concept of a balanced management approach in US law. The Act required the 'management of all the renewable surface resources of the national forests [in such a way that] they are utilized in the combination that will best meet the needs of the American people [and] will not necessarily offer the combination of uses that will give the greatest [financial] return'.[1] A significant qualification was that the approach was to be applied only over large areas of land and not to individual woods or patches of forest. Thus not every part of a forest was expected to serve every purpose, but rather the forest as a whole was. The Act also reinforced the principle of 'sustained yield', a concept that was famously pioneered in the US by Gifford Pinchot at the beginning of the nineteenth century.

It requires a fair leap in thinking to compare the American situation to that in Britain. The ecological and historical differences between the national forests of the US and forests in Britain could hardly be greater. Yet it is the kernel of the idea of multiple use that interests us here and which started to make an impact in planning circles in Britain in the 1960s. It seemed to solve the problem of fitting recreational use within the intensively managed countryside of Britain. Could the recreational use of the land be accommodated alongside the established land uses like agriculture and forestry? Nan Fairbrother, in her book *New Lives, New Landscapes*, thought it could and should:

> multiple use of our limited land is [an] inevitable development, though still only warily accepted. But though the traditional attitude of one patch one user and a notice saying PRIVATE is a simple solution where land is plentiful, Britain is too small for a no-trespassers complex whether private or public, and in future we shall need more valid reasons for keeping the world at bay than a mild paranoia.[2]

We shall come to our main historic interest in Fairbrother's book in Chapter 9, but here it is the generality of her thoughts on wooded scenery that is most relevant:

> [The] unrivalled power to create a convincing environment in a very small area is one of the many virtues of wooded scenery. In a 5-acre spinney we could be in the heart of a forest, and this is true of no other landscape. Five acres of farmland or downs or moorland are nothing; they are merely the unnoticed ground where we stand and look at the view beyond. To create a convincing environment in open landscape we need not 5 but 500 or even 5,000 acres.[3]

Fairbrother ventures that there is 'No need for boots and binoculars to appreciate the country' in the caption to a photograph of a picnicking couple.

The Forestry Commission can fairly claim to have been the first body to realise the great potential of woods and forests as a recreational attraction to rival the hills and the seaside. The Forest Parks that were opened up in the 1930s have already been mentioned in Chapter 3 and, by the 1960s, there were six of them covering a total area of 175,000 hectares and attracting 354,000 campers annually. In the 1960s and '70s, with the encouragement of the Countryside Acts, the Commission opened its forests everywhere for informal recreation on foot, and was given powers to provide facilities for the purpose, such as car parks, toilets and way-marked routes.

The Commission's largely coniferous forests may not have seemed the most promising starting point for a recreational initiative. But while newly planted forests can seem impenetrable and dull, the older forests – with their older, well-thinned woods – were coming into their own by the 1960s and '70s, and attracted thousands of people. That did not mean that the Commission saw the recreational use of forests as being on an equal footing with its statutory purpose of timber production, but a timid start to their recreational use had been made. In came 'welcome' notices at the forest edges. Interesting way-marked trails and paths were carved through the forests, bridges put up across streams, picnic places set out at viewpoints and hides erected for viewing wildlife. The very informality of a woodland walk added to the pleasure: no long preparations were needed, no backpacks and no maps, and there was something different to see at each time of year. By 1969 ninety-two forest trails had been created, together with 104 picnic sites.

At the leading edge of the Commission's recreational activity in the late 1960s was Grizedale Forest, situated between the Lakes Coniston and Windermere in the Lake District. Grizedale had not attracted the opposition that was voiced against the tree planting in Eskdale in the mid-1930s, situated, as it is, in the smoother and less rugged southern part of the Lake District, away from the central fells. By the 1960s the first Grizedale plantings were approaching maturity and the forest's position in one of the greatest tourist areas of Britain presented an exceptional opportunity to develop the forest as a multi-purpose resource.

So it appeared to foresters Dick Chard and Bill Grant, whose enlightened thinking did much to pioneer the idea of 'forests for people' in the 1960s. Grant had travelled on a Winston Churchill Memorial Travelling Fellowship to the United States to learn how foresters there had succeeded in bringing the multiple uses and values of the forest to public consciousness.[4] People in the US were encouraged to think of 'our forests', and forest rangers became almost legendary figures in the eyes of young America because they looked after a national resource that people really valued. Grant wanted to emulate this approach at Grizedale. Recreational innovations included new trails and man-made tarns built for attracting wildlife, and hides for viewing it. The well-known sculpture trail was established in 1977 and bursaries were offered to budding sculptors who used the outdoor setting of the forest for creations of wood and stone and as a launch pad for their work. Grant's innovative 'Theatre in the Forest' gained a wide reputation for musical excellence, attracting artists and entertainers from around the world to perform to an intimate audience in the stunning environment of the forest. Grizedale became one of the leading visitor attractions in the Lake District and a model for other forests to follow.

Thus, from a position in which very little woodland in Britain was open to the public in the 1960s (other than Forest Parks), the Commission, by opening its forests generally to the public, quickly became the country's principal woodland recreation provider. Contrast, however, the fairly quiet recreational use of forests in the 1960s and '70s with the highly active sports enjoyed in forests today. In the 1980s and '90s, the development of more active physical sports found a home in the generally robust, sheltered, varied and intimate environment of the planted forest. Orienteering and trail biking became popular at Grizedale and in many other areas. And for their followers and enthusiasts, some of the larger forests provided venues for more 'extreme' sports such as husky sled racing (see Picture 37) and cross-country skiing.

The Late 1970s – Felling, Windthrow and Restructuring

While recreational usage of the forests was increasing in the 1970s, the growing maturity of the new forests had many implications for the way they were managed and how they were renewed and regenerated after felling for timber. To some readers this may seem a rather arcane subject. But methods of tree management have many implications for people's pleasure in woods, whether they are seen by a recreational user seeking a varied and interesting tree environment inside the forest, or from the point of view of a tourist looking at the forest from outside.

A 'clearcutting' or 'clearfelling' approach is the norm in Britain and, as the terms imply, this means that all the trees in a section of forest are cut down at the same time. In some ways, this approach can be likened to the large-scale natural disturbances (like forest fires and insect damage) that are perfectly normal phenomena in some parts of the world. The method is favoured for its simplicity and economic advantages but disliked by many people for provoking an unwelcome change in the look of the forest and leaving ugly scars, even if the untidiness of the disturbance lasts for only a few years. Clearfelling is not a choice determined by economics alone. The silvicultural needs of the trees to be planted are considered by foresters as well. Most kinds of trees used in forestry are what ecologists call 'pioneers'. Pioneer tree species grow best in good light conditions and therefore prefer open planting sites not overtopped by other trees.

The clearfelling system contrasts with 'shelterwood cutting' and 'selective cutting', sometimes referred to as 'continuous cover' methods. These are ways of managing forests where some of the tree cover is preserved over the ground when tree felling takes place. Selective felling means that the felling takes place in small gaps or clearances and that any tree replanting necessary is similarly confined to small areas. Although practised occasionally in Britain, the methods still have to prove themselves for use on a large scale, particularly in upland forests. They have become a topic of keen interest to researchers in recent times.

An important influence on forests is windthrow. For a country that is otherwise blessed with good conditions for growing trees, the tendency of our oceanic climate towards high wind and storms is unfortunate. Trees, for all their remarkable resistance to high winds, can blow over or even snap off in stormy conditions. In the more vulnerable uplands, normal winter gales are treated very much as 'business as usual', and to some extent damage can be mitigated by planning and improved forest design. Much rarer are what foresters refer to as 'catastrophic' storms which, because of their severity and extensive regional scale, can cause major economic loss and wreak havoc on the look of the landscape. Still fresh in the minds of many people in the south-east of England is the Great Storm that struck that normally well-ordered and temperate part of the country in 1987 (see Chapter 8).

A new approach to forest management was developed at Kielder Forest in the late 1970s[5] and has been widely copied. Called 'restructuring' (see Picture 25), it involved redesigning a forest's layout and structure from first principles, aiming to move away from the early uniformity. It was hoped to limit wind damage by identifying robust internal boundary features that would help to create a permanent framework for the forest. There are more open spaces in a restructured forest and, because of the introduction of broadleaves to improve structural permanence, more edges and more varied habitats for wildlife. Permanent 'riperian' zones were created along stream sides to check erosion and improve aquatic life, and a start was made on the creation of patches of 'old growth' by leaving trees to become senile to encourage the rich biodiversity associated with old trees.

The 1980s and '90s – Wildlife

The relationship between afforestation and wildlife is a disputed subject in some quarters. Not enough time has passed to provide well-researched answers. While early ecologists like Fraser Darling were positive about the long-term ecological benefits of afforestation, conservationists in the 1980s found little to applaud about it. Conservation writers concentrated on comparing the natural history of planted forests with that of ancient or semi-natural woodland, highlighting the very obvious differences. But as Avery and Leslie point out in *Birds and Forestry*, commercial forests do not 'masquerade' as imitation natural forests and ought to be judged as a new habitat in their own right.[6]

Birds, more than other kinds of wildlife, played a telling part in forest history in the 1980s and '90s, both through 'political' events like the Flow Country and, more positively, by ongoing research to improve the structure of forests for birds.[7] Though it is a controversial point among conservationists, the richness of bird life in a forest has often been seen as the litmus test of its ecological health. There must be some element of truth in this because birds exploit many ecological niches, so reflecting the variety of insect, mammal and plant life to be found in the various parts of the forest. It is also true that bird populations are better researched than other forms of wildlife and in some cases are the only indicators of improving biodiversity that ecologists and foresters have. The idea of birds as gauges of biodiversity in forests was a useful principle; what was good for birds was thought to be good for wildlife generally.

Avery and Leslie have much to say in their book on the pros and cons of afforestation in relation to birds. They asked if it is really true, as often speculated, that threatened moorland species were replaced only by common songbirds? The conclusions are revealing and, as the authors observed, by no means in line with the popular mythology that had grown up. 'Conifer specialists', such as the goshawk, firecrest, siskin and crossbill, had widely colonised the older, planted forests. Birds of open country, on the other hand, were by no means completely eliminated. An example of this is at Thetford in the Breckland, where two declining species, the woodlark and the nightjar, have colonised the patchwork of regeneration sites – the so-called restocks – in numbers that are not far short of the original heathland populations. The authors then looked at four regional case studies where the bird populations were put in a wider context.[8] On balance, Avery and Leslie judged that Thetford had become a friendlier environment for birds than either the adjoining agriculture or the surviving areas of heathland in the Brecks. Other case studies in the book showed mixed results. The authors thought that forestry had, on balance, enriched the bird life of the North York Moors, taking account of the existing distribution of land use between forest and heathland. But in Galloway too high a proportion of the region had been afforested to be beneficial to birds, while in the Flow Country their assessment of the effect of afforestation was unequivocally negative, as noted in the last chapter.

One great birder and conservation professional to put a foot in the forestry camp was John Morton Boyd, previously mentioned for his involvement in the Flow Country. Boyd, in 1985, was the newly retired head of the NCC in Scotland and his appointment to the Forestry Commission was meant to do for nature conservation what Sylvia Crowe had done for landscape between 1963 and 1975. Boyd's approach to his consultancy work, however, differed from that of Crowe. She was one for casework – inspecting, challenging, drawing sketches and reviewing planting designs – while Boyd in the Commission (as he admitted in his autobiography) was not one for detail. It was the vision that counted – the 'greening of forestry' as he liked to call it.

As we now know from his autobiography, Boyd's 'absconding' to the Forestry Commission was resented by some of his former colleagues in the NCC. But his appointment was timely, making good use of his charismatic advocacy at a moment of rapid change for both forestry and nature conservation. In an amendment to the Wildlife and Countryside Act in 1985, the Commission was required 'to endeavour to achieve a reasonable balance between the interests of forestry and those of the environment'. This was an important new responsibility with far-reaching implications, applying not just to the management of the state forests by the Commission, but to its various functions in support of and regulation of private forestry. The statutory conservation bodies, for their part, in the mid-1980s, were also getting to grips with a statutory broadening of their role. Under the influence of European legislation, two new designations for wildlife in the wider countryside were instigated: Special Areas for Conservation, a designation for habitats and species, and Special Protection Areas, which provided added protection for rare birds.

Towards Sustainable Development

There was more than a hint of America's Multiple Use Act in the important new 'balancing' responsibility imposed on the Forestry Commission under the amendment to the Wildlife and Countryside Act. Enlightened demonstrations of multiple use of the kind described in this chapter had not been adopted everywhere, and in 1985 foresters were struggling to keep up with a drift of public opinion that often seemed to put the aesthetic and non-material needs of society ahead of economic benefits. What indeed *was* a 'reasonable balance' under the Act and how did it apply to commercial forests?

There was no definitive answer to the question which is fundamentally a political one. In Chapter 9, however, we shall come to a new era of 'sustainable development' with its implication that economic, social and environmental aspects of tourist management should be considered together. A sea change was signalled with sustainable development. Social and environmental objectives were no longer to be regarded as constraints on production in the way that they had been in the 1960s and '70s, but as objectives to be aimed for in their own right.

7

FREEDOM TO ROAM?

It was really no surprise that a government committed to privatisation should turn its attention to the Forestry Commission, even if it was small on the scale of potential candidates and seen, perhaps, as little more than a box on the government's 'for sale' list to be ticked. Nevertheless, when the Thatcher government took powers to sell Commission forests in 1981, it was not the insignificant proposal it might have seemed, since the Commission looked after around 5 per cent of the land surface of Britain, and issues of landownership were always going to be politically sensitive. The heady mix of property rights and the ongoing pressure to open up the countryside that had begun with the Countryside Acts in the late 1960s were bound to create controversy. Nearly forty years on from the end of the Second World War, there had never been a test of public attitudes towards the Forestry Commission, so its potential privatisation was unquestionably going to be a first.

We must remind ourselves here that the Commission carried out two discrete functions: first as a forest authority charged with promoting and 'policing' forestry generally and paying grants to landowners; and secondly as an agency responsible for running the state forests – the forest enterprise. What was immediately at stake was the forest enterprise. The distinction, however, was lost in much of the press comment and perhaps among some of the politicians too. Yet it was more than a simple case of journalistic broad-brush. The forestry authority was too small to survive as a department of government on its own, and to many people the talk of privatisation was an attack on forests and forestry as a whole.

This is a good moment to look at forest ownership. In 1919, the woodland resource of Britain had been almost all privately owned by the traditional landed proprietors. Out of an estimated national forest area of 1.10 million hectares at that time, only around 5 per cent was publicly owned, which was made up partly by the crown woods. By 1980 that picture had substantially altered. The forest area had increased to 2.05 million hectares, of which about *half* was in public ownership, the largest component of change being the purchase of hill land by the Commission and its afforestation. Although the period from 1919 to 1980 had been one of great change in landownership, the main political parties had shared a common approach to the development of a mixed economy of private and state forestry.

The Institute of Economic Affairs was quick off the mark with its paper *State Forestry for the Axe*, published in August 1981.[1] Its economist author, Robert Miller, saw forestry as one of those activities 'which are revealed on analysis as unimpeachable ... but with unidentifiable benefits'. The Adam Smith Institute added to the rhetoric, arguing that the public sector, now relieved of the task of creating and maintaining a strategic wood reserve, should be sold off: 'If we privatise the Forestry Commission ... we would be selling it as a going concern, not dependent on subsidies, not dependent on grants, but sold at the price at which it can operate economically.'[2] But if, as the Adam Smith Institute suggested, forestry could operate 'economically' as an out-and-out commercial activity in the private sector, why had it declined in the nineteenth century? And why had almost all European countries – despite their varied social history and environmental circumstances – evolved a mixed economy of private and public forests? The European Community countries as a whole had an aggregate *public* forest area of 38 per cent. Even in Finland and Sweden, with their highly developed commercial timber economies, there was a significant public forest estate of about 30 per cent.

The year 1981 was a tricky time to be adding to the trends of commercialism on the land. The new decade would reveal a softening of attitudes to the productivity of the post-war period. The 1981 Wildlife and Countryside Act strengthened the statutory protection of wildlife. The problem of food surpluses was leading the EU down the path of less intensive and more environmentally friendly farming practices. Environmentalist authors, such as Marion Shoard in her 1980 book *The Theft of the Countryside*, were actively questioning 'the destiny' of the countryside and arguing for its opening up. Most significant of all for forestry was the government's decision to give the Forestry Commission its so-called 'balancing duty' mentioned in the previous chapter. Had its significance for the forest sales programme been missed? For instance, would the new owners of forests continue to allow public access and would they promote wildlife conservation in the way that the Forestry Commission had done?

Seemingly, it was the reaction of the forest *users* during the committee stages of the Forestry Bill in 1981 that decided the government on a policy of piecemeal disposal of Commission woods, rather than the wholesale privatisation that was mooted for other state enterprises in the 1980s. The timber merchants, the recreational users of the forests and the nature conservation interests would all have something to say. Assurances were given that the Commission would itself decide on the woods to be sold and would implement the government's new powers to dispose of land in a 'sensible and controlled way'. The Commission was instructed to sell woods and forests under the framework of an ambiguous set of 'disposal guidelines' that were designed to calm sensitivities and offend no one.[3] The disposals, it was said, would take account of public access and the interests of nature conservation but would not compromise the development of the wood industry or threaten employment in socially fragile areas. Then again, the taxpayer would benefit because the sales would improve efficiency and raise money for the Treasury. The Forestry Commission in 1981, given the job of dismantling its own estate, was handed a very hot potato.

The institutional interest in buying forests that we encountered in Chapter 5 (in connection with company forestry) had very much cooled by the early 1980s. When in 1982 four substantial forests of around 1,000 hectares (Brycheiniog, near Brecon, Raera in west Scotland, Greystoke on the fringes of the Lake District and Leithope on the eastern edge of Roxburghshire) were advertised for sale, they attracted only scant interest from institutional buyers. Seemingly the Commission gave up on this market and focused its energies instead on selling smaller woods selected with the aim of rationalising its landholding to improve efficiency. After over sixty years of existence, it was responsible for nearly 10,000 individual woods of varying size. This approach worked better because smaller woods attracted more buyers. Hundreds of individual woods of all kinds were offered up for sale: coniferous, broadleaved and mixed woods, woods from a few acres to hundreds of acres. A typical buyer was the local farmer or neighbouring estate owner who saw the opportunity to add to his or her existing landholding, perhaps for sporting use or small-scale wood production, or merely to stop it from falling into unsympathetic hands.

In 1984 there was an unexpected Antipodean stimulus to the programme of forest sales in Britain. A newly elected and reform-minded Labour government in New Zealand was contemplating the disposal of state assets to reduce the country's budget deficit.[4] The proposals included the 'hiving off' of the planted *Pinus radiata* forests, together with the state-owned sawmills, into what at first was expected to be a state-owned forestry corporation managed at arm's length from the government. The expectation was that the corporation would return a commercial profit to the treasury of that country when it was freed of social objectives and public-service 'red tape'. Events in New Zealand were keenly watched by merchant banks in Britain and prompted inquiring visits to that country from selling agents in Britain and, in 1988, from the House of Commons Agriculture Committee.

Much might be said about the comparison of British forests with those in New Zealand, but the factor to stand out was one of difference rather than similarity. Over 80 per cent of the forest resources of that country were native forests of Podocarps and Southern beech (*Nothofagus*) which served conservation needs and provided recreational services for a population of only 3.5 million people. The Radiata forests, in contrast, amounted to just 17 per cent of New Zealand's forest resource. And since the authorities there had operated almost a locked-gate policy within these forests, their disposal by the state aroused little public opposition. There was nothing to compare with the extensive public usage of the mainly coniferous forests that had become the norm in Britain. The conclusion to the hiving-off proposal mentioned above had been anticipated by many people. Critics saw it as an unsatisfactory halfway house between the public and private sectors – neither one thing nor the other. In 1987, the government of New Zealand decided that, instead of corporatisation, it would sell off its planted forests in a piecemeal way to international wood-products companies.

If any stimulus to the political uncertainty about forests in Britain was needed, the unfolding story in New Zealand provided it. Early in 1986, *The Economist* publicised a 'leaked' report claiming that one of the forestry ministers, Agriculture Minister Michael Jopling, was 'preparing a secret plan to sell all the land held by the Forestry Commission in a single lot'.[5] The threat of the Jopling plan, true or not (in fact no more was heard of it), changed the mood of the forest users watching from the sidelines in Britain.

Perhaps it had been expected that the timber merchants would favour a sell-off of the forests and, potentially, the chance to get their hands on a huge supply of wood at an advantageous price? By 1986 the Commission was supplying nearly three-quarters of the whole of Britain's softwood supply to industry, and its timber supply policies were interwoven with the trade that had developed around it (see Chapter 8). Jopling, however, offered an alarming scenario: a private sector corporation exploiting a dominant wood-supply situation, unsympathetic to the established order of the trade. It would be accountable only to its shareholders and not to the public at large through government ministers. Would the forests simply be asset stripped for short-term gain rather than managed renewably for the production of a commodity that took more than fifty years to mature? And would the new owners offer for sale the same steady and increasing timber volumes that the Commission had forecast, and on which the merchants had predicated their expansion plans?

Against this background of unanswered questions, the timber trade closed ranks to oppose the disposals and to question the merit of making further capital investment in their factories if privatisation went ahead. One of the largest wood purchasers, the Finnish-owned Caledonian Paper Company, threatened to abandon its plans for an expansion of its Ayrshire factory, a spokesman saying 'we cannot make such an investment against an insecure background of [wood] supply'.[6]

The environmental voluntary bodies' first reaction to the proposed sale of Commission woods had been a muted one. They at first stood on the sidelines, concerned only with safeguarding individual sites of nature conservation value. The Commission managed its SSSIs according to conservation plans agreed with the nature conservation agencies, and also maintained a series of long-established nature reserves of its own. Voluntary bodies were concerned that such protected sites would be put at risk by unsympathetic purchasers. They urged that sites should be retained in sympathetic ownership or that conservation bodies should be given privileged opportunities to acquire them.

'Sponsorship' was devised to address just this problem. The Treasury's normal rule is that public assets are sold on the open market, but this was to be an exception. The Treasury permitted not-for-profit bodies to purchase woods by *negotiation* if the purchase was sponsored by a relevant government agency which, however, had to confirm that the purchase was 'particularly in the public interest'.[7] There were benefits to both the seller and potential purchasers in this arrangement because it satisfied a common desire to preserve wildlife. And since most of the voluntary bodies wished to preserve public access, it was a guarantee of sorts for that too. The Woodland Trust was particularly active in seeking sponsorship from the two Countryside Commissions. Joyden's Wood – the only Forestry Commission property then left within the circle of the M25 motorway – was one of the numerous examples of the Trust's acquisitions under the sponsorship policy. Situated on a hilltop on the south-eastern edge of Greater London, it is much used by the public for walking and exploring its archaeological interest.

The attractions of woodland *ownership* to voluntary bodies like the Trust were compelling. Ownership provided the ultimate surety that interesting wildlife habitats would be protected from damage, as well as the opportunity to encourage new aspects of wildlife interest. There was also a timing advantage. An offer of sponsorship allowed the purchaser plenty of time to fund-raise for the acquisition – an essential pre-condition for the purchase that would have been impossible in an open bidding situation. Typically, the voluntary bodies raised funds for the purchase and management of woods through local and national appeals for money, but benefited also from grants from public bodies. The Woodland Trust's purchase of Joyden's Wood was financed by a grant of public money from the Countryside Commission and from a local 'save Joyden's Wood' appeal. An accountant might question why grants of public money paid to the trusts were returned to the Treasury as 'privatisation receipts', but to the Treasury it was perhaps enough that it got another public 'liability' off its books.

Where nature conservation bodies were, in the late 1980s, seemingly content with the way that sponsorship safeguarded their particular interests in forest disposals, the arrangements did not cater so well for the concerns of the access organisations, such as the Ramblers' Association. The Ramblers had no interest in taking on the responsibility of landownership and also wanted to see public access preserved over the totality of the Commission land being sold, not just small parts of it. Prospects that the new owners might not willingly welcome the public into the acquired woods seemed to be confirmed when photographs of 'keep out' signs began to appear in the popular press.

For many of the people who enjoyed walking in the Commission's woods, their threatened disposal to private interests alerted them to an issue that they had seen more as an academic question than one of practical consequence to them. Campaigns for a statutory right of access to land had a long history, but in the 1980s and '90s they were beginning to echo more sympathetically with the public. In 1987, the Ramblers' Association launched its Forbidden Britain campaign. At this point, the forest privatisation policy of the government made a new enemy. The Ramblers declared their opposition to the sale of the forests, which they pictured as 'so negative and destructive that it beggars belief'.[8]

By 1990, it seemed that the Commission was finding it very difficult to put forward woods for sale that did not provoke critical newspaper coverage. Every wood, however infrequently visited, suddenly had its champions and defenders. Letters to the press and demonstrations at the entrance to the woods being sold seemed to be targeted to touch the nerves of government ministers. The government's response to the rapidly slowing progress of sales was to engage the local authorities in an attempt to defuse public objections. Authorities had powers to enter into legally binding access agreements with landowners. It was suggested that if such agreements could be put into place before the woods were sold, they would bind the new owners, willingly or otherwise, to preserve access.

But the plan did not look promising from the moment it was introduced. Local authorities were unwilling to be encumbered with a problem that was not of their own making and were suspicious of the financial implications of taking on the new agreements. Many of the woods, they thought, were too remote from public places to be worth worrying about. The result was that there was little take-up of the local authority agreements; according to the Ramblers in February 1994, agreements had been made in only nineteen cases of forest sales out of 299 which they knew to be potential disposals.[9] Worse for the government, the programme of Commission sales was now burdened with another layer of delay and uncertainty, while the local authorities went through the bureaucratic motions of considering the demand for access in each and every individual case.

It seems now that it was the Ramblers' intervention that was the decisive moment in what the magazine *Country Life* later referred to as that 'inglorious privatisation debate'.[10] In 1993, the government announced a review of the future of forestry, so provoking an avalanche of articles in the popular press and outdoor activity magazines. Overwhelmed by advice and opinion from all quarters, the review group received over 4,000 representations from industry, NGOs and individuals.[11] If the review had been intended to 'out' public support for state forestry, it certainly succeeded. Even landowners who might have had other views joined the condemnation. The late Duke of Buccleuch, in 1993, had 'yet to find anyone who could see merit in the [privatisation] idea', and applauded the 'partnership of state and private sector forestry' which, he thought, 'work[ed] extremely well'.[12] In 1994, the review produced what it had promised – a clear outcome. Scottish Secretary Ian Lang, speaking in the House of Commons on behalf of the three government ministers responsible for forestry in England, Scotland and Wales, announced that the government had decided to keep the Commission's woods in the public sector 'at this stage in their development'.[13] It seems that privatisation had simply run out of steam in the face of a united front against it. 'Reason wins over political dogma', said the leader in *The Scotsman* on 11 April 1994.[14]

The Commission that came out of the review was not the same as the one that went into it. That was bound to happen. During thirteen years of uncertainty and political pressure for forest sales, there had been a revolution of thinking about the land and about land use, as will be apparent from Chapter 9. Support for the Commission's multi-purpose objectives were voiced by leading environmentalists. The National Trust's Director General, Angus Stirling, thought that 'progress towards a balanced multi-purpose role for forestry had been significant and highly creditable'.[15] Barbara Young, Chief Executive of the RSPB, considered that 'no alternative exists that guarantees success', and estimated that the government would have had to pay out £50 million annually to whoever took over the forests to ensure that the Commission's conservation and recreation policies were maintained.[16] It was hard to see either the Treasury or the landowning community commit to such a proposition.

What effect did the forest disposals actually have on public access? It might be thought that after thirteen years of selling woods and forests, the practical effect would be considerable. The selling of an estimated 180,000 hectares of state forest between 1981 and 1994 was the main change over a period that saw a reduction in the state's share of woodland ownership from 50 per cent to 37 per cent. Shoard suggested that the forest sales had had a disproportionate effect on public access because they were concentrated on the small woods that would have been especially attractive to people for walking.[17] If the Commission had sold 46 per cent of its individual woods (as the Ramblers had estimated) then, she implied, a similar proportion of its access had been lost. The implication of lost recreational opportunity might, however, be an exaggeration; it is probable that the real loss of recreational access to forests was more than counterbalanced by the many improvements to woodland access through the actions of sponsored buyers and by investments in recreational facilities made by the Commission itself in its retained forests.

Of course, the 'victory' on forest disposals was only a small part of the Ramblers' campaign for public access to the countryside. Public access remained a live political issue which was brought to Parliament when the Labour party came to power in 1997. The Countryside and Rights of Way Act, 2000 (CRoW) was not the universal right of access that some campaigners had hoped for. Like agricultural land in England and Wales, woodland was excluded from the access provisions in the legislation, although, as a sop to the campaigners, landowners could voluntarily dedicate their woods for public access if they so wished. The Forestry Commission in England and Wales did this under the legislation,[18] but few if any private estates followed suit and (more surprisingly) even charity landowners rejected it. North of the border, the Land Reform Scotland Act, 2003 provided a universal right of access to all land including forest and woodland subject to some qualifications. Thus a legal right of access now exists to *all* Commission forests in England, Scotland and Wales, in contrast to the 'privileged' freedom to roam that existed before.

Therefore, had the new access laws been in force before 1980, they would, it seems, have addressed the concerns of the Ramblers. Will this make a difference in the event of similar lurches in forest policy in the future? Today, state ownership is nearer to 30 per cent, a consequence mainly of additional tree planting by private owners and charities. It is hard to imagine that forest ownership will ever be seen again in quite the same stark terms as it was between 1981 and 1994. The question can be restated: are the state forests still delivering what people want? Forestry has acquired a new status in the sensitive global politics of climate change (see Chapters 8 and 9) and the ability of the government to lead by example in uncharted waters seems as compelling today as it ever was.

8

TIMBER FROM THE TREES

It would perhaps be warming to start this chapter by painting a David and Goliath picture of a downtrodden home timber industry surviving against all the odds a dominant import trade that had done its best to squeeze it out of existence. Perhaps there is a very small grain of truth in this. But in reality Britain's forests are far too small and fragmented to provide more than a fraction of the nation's timber needs, currently about 16 per cent. Ready availability of timber from abroad – while it hampered the case for putting money into tree growing in Britain – helped the economy. Cheap wood from abroad meant less expensive houses at home, so in a way we all benefited. Only in times of war have timber imports dried up, throwing us back on our indigenous timber supply.

We need not dwell for long on the nature of the *imported* trade. Based on God-given 'natural' sources of timber, it flourished on a diet of cheap wood, frequently coming from so-called 'concessions' granted by foreign governments to foster employment and regional development in their own countries. Each step in the historic development of transport in Britain opened the doors of the economy wider to this influx of world trade. Timber is a bulky and heavy material that is difficult and costly to move around, but thanks to the development of ports, steamships, canals and railways, the softwoods of North America and the Baltic region were imported to Britain in ever-increasing quantities. The impact of the railways on the timber industry was particularly dramatic. The tentacles of the railway companies reached into the uplands and the more isolated regions where the canal system couldn't go, opening up inland markets for wood that, until the middle of the nineteenth century, had relied almost entirely on British-grown timber.

Coincident with the development of the railway system in the middle and late nineteenth century was the adoption of free trade, a policy that lowered prices and improved the access of the importers to markets. When Colonial Preference (the policy that encouraged the development of trade with the colonies) was abolished in 1860, timber importers from across the world got unrestricted access to British markets. Canada, which in the 1850s was the source of over half of Britain's timber imports, was by 1870 supplying less than one-fifth. The Nordic and Baltic areas – Norway, Sweden, Finland and Russia – took over.

In this free-trade environment, the importing companies prospered. Middlemen between the importers and the village carpenters, joiners and house builders keenly promoted their sawn wood stocks to potential customers. In his gentle reminiscences of his grandfather's Buckinghamshire timber business, Walter Rose, in *The Village Carpenter*, describes how his grandfather witnessed the change over from English to imported timber. After 1883, the importing merchants sent their representatives to the country carpenters to solicit sales.[1] There was good money in it and the representatives were 'well-groomed men who travelled in state', later to deliver the chosen wood stocks via the extended railway system. In the years between 1850 and 1910, the volume of timber imported to Britain increased five-fold and Britain became the most important timber market in the world.

The importers provided all the things that the home trade found most difficult; consistency of supply, an unlimited quantity in a range of useful grades and sizes, and all delivered at a low price that reflected the exploitation of a natural forest. By way of contrast, the forest industry in Britain was increasingly based on a *planted* timber resource, and thus on the uncertain and changing circumstances and attitudes of Britain's many individual landowners. Many small or irregular transactions of mixed tree species did not help the cause of timber marketing and, historically, the relationship between the landowners and the wood-using industry was often a fractious or opportunist one. It was a persuasive merchant who could prevail upon a well set-up landowner to let the woodcutters in among his precious pheasants, partridge and deer.[2]

Yet, as we shall see, there were still opportunities for the aspiring home timber merchant or sawmiller. The niches they occupied were of different kinds. Some purchasers wanted custom-made products, not the standard sizes available from importers. Changes of dimensions at short notice were difficult for the importing agents to supply, as were long lengths because they were awkward for overseas mills to handle and ship. Others wanted small quantities of native timbers for specialist markets. These were the typical order book items of the domestic industry.

An Ancient Trade

The early days of woodworking and the timber trade are difficult to track down. For the origins of sawmilling we have, rather speculatively, to go back to the Romans! Adam Hart-Davies, in his book *What the Past Did For Us*, suggests that the first power saw was invented by the Romans in the Middle East. It had reciprocating blades (the cutting blades went backwards and forwards like a handsaw) and was water-powered and used for cutting slabs of stone.[3] When and if this technology was ever passed down or copied, we don't know. In medieval Britain, right through until the nineteenth century, pit-sawing of large timber – that immense and grindingly hard work – was the norm (see Picture 14). In Europe, sawmills had been developed long before the nineteenth century. The earliest mills (crude reciprocating saws in wooden frames powered by wind or water) were developed in sixteenth-century Holland and Norway for cutting 'round timber' (logs) in the importing and exporting trades.

When the idea came to Britain in the seventeenth century, it was not embraced with enthusiasm. A wind-powered sawmill was built in 1658 on the River Thames at Lambeth, but its operation was frustrated by pit sawyers who saw the machine as an unwelcome threat to their jobs and rioted. Parliament, it seems, through the influence of Cromwell, was persuaded to prohibit the mills.[4] More than a century passed before the concept was revived. In the 1760s, James Stansfield, a Yorkshire carpenter who became well known for his sawmill designs, built a wind-powered mill at Limehouse,[5] a centre for boat building on the Thames. This too ran into trouble and was closed down.

The Yorkshire connection, however, persisted. Yorkshire was a great place for innovation in machinery, and around this time we first hear of William Osborne, a timber merchant in Hull (then a major centre for timber imports), who built a wind-powered mill in 1796.[6] Osborne was one of the two Yorkshire merchants behind the Glenmore Company, which worked timber in the remote upper reaches of Strathspey in Scotland around the 1780s. Until the early eighteenth century, the pinewoods of Highland

Scotland had been largely unknown. According to the Statistical Account of Scotland, the eighteenth-century timber contractors in Speyside brought with them 'sawmills', along with 'every kind of implement and apparatus of the best and most expensive sorts'. The saws of this era were also of the reciprocating type, rather than the circular kind that came into common use later. The story continues because the Glenmore Company, at the end of the eighteenth century, built sawmills at Garmouth, the small Morayshire village where the River Spey joins the sea, 'for manufacturing the timber' after it had been floated down the river. Hedging their bets, it seems, 'The one is a windmill, and works from 36 to 40 saws. The other goes by water and works from 30 to 36 saws.'[7]

River floating and rafting of logs and rough-sawn timber was the only way to move it to distant markets before the advent of canals and railways. Linnard, in his *Welsh Woods and Forests*, mentions timber transport on the Severn, Wye, Neath, Tywi, Dyfi and Conwy.[8] In the Highlands of Scotland, the owners of the inland estates and their contracted timber merchants used river transport as the first stage of a journey to send timber to the markets in London and other towns and cities. We are fortunate to have Elizabeth Grant's entertaining eye-witness account of floating on the River Spey at Rothiemurchus in 1813:

> The logs prepared by the loppers had to be drawn by horses to the nearest running water, and there left in large quantities until the proper time for sending them down the streams. It was a busy scene all through the forest, so many rough little horses moving about in every direction, each dragging its load, attended by an active boy as guide and remover of obstructions ... This driving lasted till sufficient timber was collected to render the opening of the sluices profitable.[9]

Grant goes on to describe the life of the so-called Spey floaters who took charge of the logs when they left the boundaries of the Grant Estate. When the river was 'large' enough and free of obstructions, the logs were made up into rafts for their journey to the mouth of the river at Garmouth.

It was not only the Speyside landowners who experimented with saw-mills. In the late eighteenth and nineteenth centuries, nearly every upland estate with a suitable river followed the fashion of building a water-powered sawmill to serve its local needs for building timbers, making country furniture, farm carts, fencing and supplying the other products required by the estate carpenter and wheelwright. Generally, it was the landowners that built sawmills because it was they who owned the rivers. On the River Don in Aberdeenshire, Archibald Grant of Monymusk was one of the first to explore the idea. A great enthusiast for forestry – it is recorded that he had planted 2 million trees by 1754 – he was sharp-eyed in keeping up with the latest innovations in estate machinery. He paid £1 to a man for cutting and pit-sawing a quantity of timber in 1731, but by 1754 was planning to build water-driven sawmills.[10]

The middle of the nineteenth century saw the beginnings of the timber industry as we would recognise it today. Steam power and machine tools had started to change woodworking from an unco-ordinated rural and estate-based craft to that of a factory business, and it was *planted* woodland that was providing the volumes of useful raw material that were needed in the machine age. With those developments came a bigger role for the professional sawmiller as the middleman between the landowners and the wood users, who were the builders, farmers and makers of wooden artefacts of various kinds, and the big industries like the railways and the mines. By this time, the location of sawmills no longer depended critically on a plentiful supply of wind or water, although well-sited watermills were still in common usage. Instead, by harnessing the power of the steam engine, sawmills could be situated to connect with the railway system and an improving but still primitive road system. Steam ended the old connection between the sawmiller and the country estate, subject only to the aspiring sawmiller acquiring a convenient site on or near to a railway siding (see Picture 1).

The extending tentacles of the railway system in the last decades of the nineteenth century provided access to new areas of woodland hitherto beyond the economic reach of transport. In Scotland, sawmillers opened up what they called 'country sawmills'. These were portable mills operated by a static steam engine, housed in temporary open-sided sheds and sited by a forest roadside or in clearings in the woods. They could be moved from place to place every few months, and the woodcutters and sawyers were accommodated in temporary wooden huts which were flat-packed and moved with the job. The sawdust and waste wood produced in the milling process helped to fuel the steam engine and to provide fuel for cooking and heating the huts. Timber merchant Brownlie had a team of twenty-five men who moved from site to site in the rich vein of timber that grew on the landed estates of the eastern Borders and Berwickshire.[11] On the west coast of Scotland, merchant Adam Wilson brought in timber by 'puffer' (steamship) from the 'up-country' mills at Oban, Inveraray and Benmore to his harbour mill at Troon in Ayrshire.[12]

The published histories of these two sawmilling families offer an insight into the home-grown timber industry over the last 150 years. Brothers Alexander and Robert Brownlie, the sons of a blacksmith, acquired their sawmill site at Haughhead in the village of Earlston, Berwickshire in 1858.[13] They supplied the North British and Caledonian Railway companies with pine and larch railway sleepers, and with oak and ash planking used for the sides and floors of the rolling stock. Wilson's was one of the first timber companies to see the chance of profit in the booming coal industry.[14] As well as their Troon mill, they had one at Auchinleck at the confluence of the great network of railway lines that served the numerous Ayrshire collieries.

Timber was needed for many purposes in the mining industry and in a great number of specifications. Pit props were there to steady and control roof subsidence in the underground tunnels and galleries that formed the working infrastructure of the deep mining industry (see Picture 9). They prevented detached pieces of rock from falling and causing injury. Timber roadway supports were a permanent feature of the underground network of tunnels. Nearer the coal face, they were used as supports for the more temporary purpose of 'propping and shoring'. One of the reasons that wooden pit props were liked by underground workers was that wood gave a warning of excessive roof weight by 'talking', that is they creaked when placed under an excessive load, allowing the miners time to correct inadequate propping positions and anticipate rock fall.[15] Softwood (coniferous timber) was the preferred wood for most uses, but hardwoods (from broadleaved trees) were used for so-called chocks, wedges and other special purposes.

By way of contrast to the mainly softwood mills in Scotland, hardwood sawmilling was predominant in England and Wales, drawing its supplies from the mainly broadleaved woods and hedgerows of the landowners. Venables of Stafford became one of the leading firms of hardwood sawmillers. The story of the firm's establishment in the latter part of the nineteenth century was told by Roger Venables in 1966.[16] A jobbing joiner and builder by trade, his grandfather worked at the grand country houses in the Stafford area where his only frustration, it seems, was the landowners' reluctance to settle their bills! He accordingly offered to take standing trees in prompt payment for services rendered rather than to invoice them for cash. He bought and felled trees, produced logs and, in the manner of the day, dug a pit and started sawing them up.

Venables recalled his grandfather's hardwood markets:

Sycamore was always in demand [at] the silk mills where it was used for spools and bobbins ... and of course every household in those days had a mangle with sycamore rollers. Local shoemakers came for cutting boards in lime or beech, and press blocks in elm. The local millwrights drew on stocks of hornbeam, pearwood, holly and beech for their many wind and water mills ... Clogmakers still had yearly cuts of alder coppice, [and the pottery and glass trades] were regular buyers of hollow 'craterods' (slender bending rods of hazel used for making the woven crates). The canals were flourishing in the industrial areas of North and South Staffs [and they needed] long oak for barge building. Old felled oaks were used chiefly for roof timbers for churches and when the First World War broke out in 1914, we were busy cutting from them timbers for the roof trusses of Bristol University.

Not much is written about the history of the land that does not hanker after the romantic age of horse work. The rosy picture often conveyed of well-fed and cared-for animals seems at odds with the harsh working and living conditions of land workers of those times, yet there is no doubt of the affection that the timber merchants showed for their animal charges. Tom Smith[17] recalled the carters and horsemen at his father's timber yard at Kirkoswald, Ayrshire, in the 1930s: 'It used to be a wonderful sight to see half a dozen heavy Clydesdale horses turning out each morning, groomed to perfection with harness polished like a guardsman's boots.' And merchant Adam Wilson was of like mind, here referring to the understanding that horses had with their keepers: 'The horses, Clydesdales and Suffolk Punches, were quite accustomed, naturally, to the less printable utterances of their masters, but they were well attuned to the difficulties of handling clumsy carts, heavy chains, and irregular logs; the command "ease an inch" brought just that – an inch's relaxation of the traces as the horse backed up.'[18]

War in the Woods

The remarkable story of timber working in the two world wars is as much a human story as it is the political and strategic one described in earlier chapters. Ignorance rather than incompetence appears to have characterised the conduct of timber operations in the First World War. Their planning was on shaky ground from the beginning; there were no statistics on domestic timber stocks, no indication of location, species, sizes and conditions, how much there was or how to harvest it. All that existed were official Board of Agriculture figures giving the acreage of woods in different counties which were based on surveys that were never claimed to be more than crude estimates and, as one forestry expert put it, were 'widely held to be wrong'. Furthermore, the various parts of the industry – the sawmillers, the timber hauliers, the felling contractors and the landowners – had little experience of working together. In contrast to the paucity of information on the home trade, it was said that information on *imported* timber was known right down to the last plank.

The slow build-up of the resources needed for wartime timber production has already been noted (Chapter 2). Only in the second half of 1915 was some real urgency given to home production. The big problem was a shortage of men and horses. The men had gone into the army and the army had requisitioned most of the horses that had been working on the land. The extraction of timber was not easily hurried in an age when horses were the main engine of the rural economy. When the wartime government complained of slow progress, the timber merchants responded with equal irritation about the lack of resources to speed things up.

In 1916, the government took an energetic grip of things. Wood fellers, hauliers and sawmill workers were designated as 'reserved occupations', which meant that they could no longer be conscripted into the army or transferred to other industries. They appealed for thousands of extra workers by asking Canada and other countries for help. The first of many Canadian companies arrived in the spring of that year, setting up camp at Virginia Water in Surrey. The Canadians, a military unit, were deployed throughout the country from Southampton to Inverness, and in France. Civilian timber workers came from Newfoundland (then a crown colony) and from Finland and Portugal. The government, meanwhile, started up its own timber harvesting operations which, in 1917, became the Board of Trade Timber Supply Department. As well as producing timber, the department co-ordinated the activities of the overseas workers and recruited a Women's Forestry Corps as an off-shoot of the Women's Land Army (see Picture 3).

George Ryle, in his book *Forest Service*, gives a glimpse of the huge scale of the department's timber work at the close of 1917.[19] Including the overseas units, it had 15,000 men and women working in it, as well as running 182 sawmills. The mills were not the permanent factory structures of today, but 'country mills' of the kind described earlier. As befitted the larger scale of operations in their home country, the Canadian mills – shipped over from Canada with the men – had a large appetite for timber. The apocryphal story is told of one heavy-handed Canadian unit posted to Ayrshire to produce timber. They were said to have used up all of the standing timber they had come to fell for the construction of their own base camp and sawmill![20]

With the setting up of the Timber Supply Department, measures were introduced to control the allocation of timber to the various wartime markets. The War Office placed controls on tree felling and fixed the price of wood, which by then had 'gone through the roof' thanks to buoyant demand. Comfortable with their own familiar way of doing things, the controls were resented by the fiercely independent timber companies that provided the bulk of the resources. Timber merchant William Wilson, who, according to the Wilson family history, was of a forceful nature:

> embellished with a dour sense of humour … never found it less than irksome to work to any schedule not of his own making, but that was exactly what was required of him by the Ministry of Supply for the duration of the Great War … whether the timbers were ordered directly by the Ministry, or simply with the Ministry's approval, the Ministry it was who issued licences to cover every step from cutting down the tree to selling the wood.[21]

Four hundred members of the Timber Trades Federation gathered at a meeting in October 1917 to protest against the overbearing grip of the department and to urge on the government a demand that the hated arrangements be stopped immediately after the war.[22]

The effect of all this central direction was dramatic. Demand for timber overwhelmed the woodcutters as timber imports dried up and landowners responded to appeals to sell their standing timber for the war effort. Estate woods that had never produced anything in living memory other than timber for odd-jobbing were opened up for the first time. With the shortage of horses, improvisation took over. Steam engines were too heavy and cumbersome to move about 'off-road', but could winch in bundles of felled trees from a road or track (see Picture 2), either pulling them directly over the ground or carrying them suspended from aerial ropeways. There are records, for instance, of a ropeway on the Lovat Estate, near Beauly, and another on the duchy estate at Brimpts on Dartmoor. The tree trunks at Brimpts were carried by cableway 5 miles across the moor to Princetown station. Elsewhere, temporary railway tracks were laid for horse-pulled timber carriages (see Picture 4). In the Highlands, timber floating enjoyed a brief resurgence as every possible means was used to get logs out of the forest and into the mills.

Another War, Another Wood Goes Down

Echoes of the First World War were still reverberating when war broke out again in 1939. Quietly, the government had been planning for this moment and there was none of the 'fumbling' that had characterised the arrangements for timber supply in the First World War.[23] Not enough time had elapsed for the Forestry Commission's oldest forests to come into production so appeals were again made to the landowners to offer timber. A government department was set up to supplement timber supply under the over-arching control of a Timber Control authority. Frank House, an official of the Timber Control, writing in his 1965 book *Timber at War*, commented on:

> The remarkable part which wood and wood manufactures played during the war effort [which] was achieved by the timber trade throughout the country virtually closing down as commercial units and becoming servants, or more exactly an integral part, of a Government Department. The machinery of this amazing metamorphosis was that of the Timber Control Department of the Ministry of Supply.[24]

One of the functions of the Timber Control Department was to purchase standing timber. In a search for pit wood, Anstace Goodhart, a lumberjill, was instructed to look at every wood marked on the map as having conifers in it. 'It is generally obvious', she wrote, 'from the first few minutes whether the owner falls into category A (those who are helpful) or category B (those who definitely aren't), [but] persistence on the point that the timber really is vital to the war effort generally wins the day.'[25] Hanging in the air was the unvoiced threat of compulsory acquisition of the timber if owners desisted. With a humorous recollection of some of the 'category B' landowners that he had encountered, George Ryle (recalling his service in the timber production department in South Wales) remembered that cases of compulsory purchase came to mind only because of their rarity.[26]

Crude Expediency and Brute Hard Work

Russell Meiggs, introduced in Chapter 3, recounts that an astonishing 73,100 men and women were employed at the peak of the wartime timber production, compared to fewer than 15,000 at the outbreak of the war.[27] It was a struggle to find recruits; 'crude expediency and brute hard work' is how Meiggs described the forest work. Forestry and sawmill workers were again designated as reserved occupations along with agricultural workers. To a nucleus of experienced merchants, estate workers and contractors were added civvy street recruits, volunteers from all over the world, prisoners of war and even schoolboys and their teachers on work parties at 'holiday' camps (see Picture 8).

Anyone interested in life at the 'sharp end' of forest operations in the war can do no better than read the numerous reminiscences of the lumberjills that have been published over the years, well illustrated with their treasured Box Brownie pictures. Fresh from the action, as it were, *Meet the Members* in 1945 told the unadorned 'plain story'[28] of the Women's Timber Corps (WTC), intended to rebut the glamour image that had been portrayed of them in the wartime newspapers. Set up in the spring of 1942 and created initially from a core of the Land Army women already working in forestry, the WTC drew its inspiration from the Women's Forestry Corps in the First World War. Recruitment made rapid progress and by the middle of 1943 there were 6,000 members. The transformation from hairdresser, typist or shop assistant to professional tree feller or saw-bench assistant must have been a traumatic one. John McEwen, who was briefly employed as an instructor at the Scottish training centre at Shandford Lodge, near Brechin, described in later years his concern for the well-being of his charges:

> I can never forget seeing these girls going home at night, dead beat and hardly able to walk, after working a whole day from 8 in the morning until 5 at night, using axes and saws which were quite new to them … The girls were nearly all town girls, I met only two out of the dozens I came across, who were country girls and could look after themselves, more or less.[29]

After training the women were dispersed all over the country to work in the Timber Department's far-flung operations, or in twos and threes in trade sawmills and alongside private estate workers.

Not Forgotten

'There'll be praise for every service, and medals by the score, for all except that noble band, the forgotten Timber Corps.' So goes a verse in an anonymous poem[30] that drew attention to the low-key recognition given to the corps during and at the end of the war. Along with the women of the Land Army, they felt aggrieved that their services to the nation had not received the recognition that was given to the armed forces through, for instance, invitations to armistice events. The lumberjills' story had a postscript in 2007, when an 'official' commemorative medal was struck for them and a statue erected at Aberfoyle in Perthshire (see Picture 10).

The Canadians, for example, were received by King George VI and Queen Elizabeth at Balmoral in 1941. In contrast to their wide-ranging deployment in the First World War, they worked exclusively in the north and north-east of Scotland in the Second World War. This was because the private estates of the Highlands and Grampians were the only places in the country to offer the prospect of the really concentrated timber work that would properly use their expertise and capacity for work.

Major G.F.G. Stanley's contemporary account of the Canadian logging work in Scotland explains that the men found the work in the pinewoods of the Highland estates particularly congenial because they were more akin a 'heavily wooded park' than the thick and tangled virgin forests of their own country that they were used to.[31] Not much was overlooked in their preparations. They came as an 'all-found' package complete with their own sawyers, millwrights, mechanics, lumberjacks, camp cooks, electricians, shoemakers, tailors, carpenters and so on, together with medical orderlies and the equipment needed for erecting their camps and sawmills. 'On the whole', Stanley wrote, 'one may say that each forestry company is equipped on the basis of the most up-to-date methods of logging used in eastern Canada, with a few special items from the West.' The Canadian methods and machines for timber extraction, road-building and sawmilling were a source of astonishment in the Highland estates which, in the 1940s, were still in the era of handcarts and horses. The camps included one at Berriedale in Caithness; the diary entry for 4 November 1943 of one of the Berriedale Canadians reads: 'The last tree of commercial value left standing in Caithness was felled today at 15.45 hours and three cheers were given by the men.'[32]

Altogether 7,000 men were employed in the Canadian camps at the peak of production, the railway stations of Aviemore, Carrbridge and Kingussie becoming the hub for the sorting and transport of timber to the coalfields and southern markets. Other countries swelled the numbers of woodsmen and sawmillers from overseas.[33] The Newfoundlanders were a voluntary civilian unit recruited by radio appeal in their home country and, by the end of January 1940, amounted to a force of 2,150 men. Their seventy-one separate work locations ranged from the New Forest to Yorkshire and to the far north of Scotland. Australia and New Zealand sent engineer units; the New Zealanders operated thirteen sawmills in such locations as Cirencester in Gloucestershire, Savernake in Wiltshire and Petersfield in Hampshire.

From Belize to Gourock

But surely the most unlikely of the wartime timber deployments were the volunteers from British Honduras (now Belize) who came to Scotland 'at the end of the mahogany season'. If the shock of their transition from tropical America to the woods of the eastern Scottish Borders – via a seventeen-day sea journey from Belize to Gourock on the Clyde – was not enough in itself, they arrived in the middle of the winter, in January 1941, and (as one of their number recalled) 'had to go to work ... right off to the forest the very next day knee deep in snow' (see Picture 7).[34] The Duke of Sutherland fired off a broadside when he heard that a *second* party of Hondurans was being posted (in November 1942) to a camp at Golspie in Sutherland, where his family seat, Dunrobin Castle, was being used as a military hospital. In a speech in the House of Lords, the duke referred to it as 'sheer lunacy' that the men should be sent to Dunrobin to face 'the rigours of a northern Highland winter, in contrast to the Canadians who were accustomed to such'.[35]

It is easy to assume that the technical advances to which foresters are now accustomed were available during the war, but generally it was axes, handsaws and horses that were the main working tools of the forest. Chainsaws had been introduced in the 1930s but were too heavy and cumbersome for everyday use, while the early farm tractors were generally too light for extracting timber. Improvisation was the order of the day; every wheel and winch rusting away in estate workshops and blacksmiths' yards was pressed into service. Log chutes, overhead cableways and narrow-gauge railways were put back to work, the loaded timber wagons now pulled along by small diesel tugs. Conditions were basic and there were constant interruptions from breakdowns. Traditionalists looked askance at the arrival of new-fangled mechanical equipment and struggled to make it work. McEwen recalled how horses and tractors worked together extracting timber to a roadside in Angus in 1942:

> The surface was never broken and the entire horse section of the job went like clock-work … It was very different with the tractor section. Even on the harder ground, getting bogged down was quite frequent, and the loading bay became [such a] quagmire … that the … measurers had to be supplied with thigh length waders.[36]

The Hardwood Industry

We must move on to the timber markets after the two world wars. Many woodland crafts had enjoyed a revival during the war years, but when Herbert Edlin wrote his *Woodland Crafts in Britain* in 1949, he was sounding the last post on many of them. The snapshot of late Victorian hardwood sawmilling noted above illuminates only one strand of the timber market story. Manual crafts like hewing, cleaving, turning and weaving transformed wood into artefacts that never went near a sawmill, and coppice work was the main source of such material. The great survivors of the coppice industries were the hazel and sweet chestnut coppices that were used for making hurdles and fencing, crafts which persist even today on a small scale in the south and south-east of England. One landowner who found a market for his hazel coppice in the 1930s was Lord Montague at Beaulieu. His agent Captain H. Widnell noted that his lordship could make no money from farm rentals, but instead made enough from the coppices to keep the estate going in difficult times: 'we made what money we could out of cutting our coppices to supply the hazel wood industry, or felling trees on the natural regeneration plan.'[37]

Markets, of course, were key to work in the forest; when markets for small roundwood and coppice products disappeared, the traditional ways of working the woods died out. Hand tools and pole-lathes were retired and broken up, and the coppices were neglected, either allowed to develop into 'high forest' or replanted with different kinds of tree. The brutal supply and demand equation impacted just as much on timber as it did on the coppice products. At the end of the First World War there had been no doubt that the timber importers would resume their normal assertiveness. Overseas countries were keen to earn foreign currency in a world that was fast moving into recession. The government's return to its pre-war free-trade policy meant that timber came flooding into the ports, and prices for the hard-pressed timber merchants at home collapsed.

In Chapters 2 and 4 we saw how the break-up of many landed estates after the First World War resulted in a glut of property sales. The purchase of some of the estates by developers provided a lifeline for the timber merchants. The distressed sale of oaks, beeches, elms, ash and sycamores – trees grown to large sizes in the parks and policy woods of the estates – provided a once-in-a-lifetime opportunity to buy timber that, in ordinary times, would never have been put up for sale. Timber merchants viewed the sale of the estates with mixed feelings, always grateful for the opportunity to buy cheap timber in a keenly competitive market, but well aware that forced sales were probably the last thing to stimulate the new tree planting that was needed to sustain their industry into the future. There was, unfortunately, no choice; it was a question of benefiting now and regretting at leisure.

The pattern of estate break-up continued in the same vein after the Second World War. By then most of the 'best' hardwoods had been winkled out from the woods for the wartime markets. Hardwood tree felling is often described as 'selective' and, when all the straightest and most valuable trees are removed, it is referred to as 'creaming'. This left behind a wood that was 'gappy' and, from the point of view of the timber merchant, of indifferent quality. Timber merchants wondered where their future supplies were coming from. Maturing trees were hard to find because there had been little broadleaved planting in the second half of the nineteenth century.

The situation said everything about why forestry differs from manufacturing or farming. More growing timber was something that money couldn't buy. Broadleaves take sixty years or more before they start to produce timber and no amount of capital investment or 'digging for Britain' could make any difference. Unfortunately, small quantities of trees do not justify large amounts of investment. The capital needed to enter the new factory-based world of furniture, flooring and joinery was beyond the means of most of the small, dispersed and independently minded British merchants, and a visit to half a dozen hardwood mills was described by one sawmilling expert as 'almost a review of the history of the development of wood-working machinery'.[38]

Britain Can Make It

An illustration of the problem of hardwood supply was the Chilterns furniture industry. Furniture making, one of the great traditional uses of hardwood timber, was poised to enjoy a huge expansion after the Second World War. In High Wycombe, at the centre of the beechwood industry, there were 138 firms making furniture in 1972. One of the household names in furniture was (and still is) Ercol, well known for its 'Windsor' furniture range, first shown to the public at the 1946 'Britain Can Make It' exhibition. In his book *A Furniture Maker*, Lucian Ercolani tells how he was approached by the Board of Trade towards the end of the war to help supply 'utility furniture', an initiative to supply low-cost furniture in functional designs for the retail market.[39]

Ercolani understood the implication of what he was about to take on. 'I knew that the Windsor chair had been made largely in our countryside, with timber which appeared to be dry but which was not dry enough for furniture – or even dry enough to enable two pieces to be joined together.' The Board wanted him to make 100,000 Windsor chairs, with a contract for another 100,000 to follow. He realised that he would have to develop factory methods and, for the first time, used kiln-dried wood: 'with our new methods it would be a matter of a few seconds instead of hours for a chair, which would be of better quality.'

The Ercolani family, it must be said, did not give up on native timbers, but persevered, introducing drying kilns and overcoming the practical challenges of successfully drying and machining hardwood timber. Elm – one of the two timbers used for making his company's flagship product, the Windsor chair – is durable and tough, but its susceptibility to warping and shake made it difficult to 'tame' for mechanised processes. The greatest problem, however, was not so much one of technique, but of quantity. Almost as soon as imports were resumed after the war, the timber for Ercolani's factory was coming from overseas, supplied to the furniture factories by large out-of-town timber yards carrying importers' stock from all over the world. And when Dutch elm disease struck in the 1970s it finally put paid to any thoughts of long-term continuity in the supply of elm timber for furniture making. Around 30 million mainly hedgerow elms were killed in an unfolding tree catastrophe that was keenly felt, particularly in parts of the south of England where the English elm lent a unique character to the landscape. By 1977, 92 per cent of the elms in the south and south-east of England were dead.

Hard on the heels of Dutch elm disease came the Great Storm, a tree disaster that, on this occasion, destroyed 15 million trees in a single night! On the morning of 16 October 1987, the population of south-east England awoke to a scene of complete devastation. The idea that nature could inflict such a vicious blow on the settled landscape of mainly parks, gardens and street trees, coupled with the sudden and completely unexpected nature of the event, turned the storm into what was probably the most recorded one-off tree event of all time. People were trapped in their homes by fallen trees and lives were lost in the dangerous job of clearing roads and gardens, electricity cables and green spaces. The storm uprooted twice as many broadleaved trees as would normally have been harvested for timber over a two-year period across the whole of Britain. Short-term timber feasts inspire a flurry of activity to find new timber markets, but time is not on a merchant's side. Timber deteriorates when it is left to lie on the ground and the industrial capacity to use it to good effect is quickly swamped. So many of the best logs of oak, sweet chestnut, beech and sycamore went to continental Europe for veneers and furniture making, and much more went into low-value markets in Britain, like pallet blocks and firewood.

What of oak, the characteristic tree of Britain and, potentially at least, the most important commercial hardwood timber? Herbert Edlin in the 1960s described it as the problem tree of British forestry because it was difficult to find trees good enough to satisfy the construction and building trades which were its most important markets.[40] For every good tree that was found, twenty others were of poor quality, and markets for low-quality oak were in rapid decline. Nevertheless, in the last quarter of the twentieth century, the demand for oak benefited from a flurry of barn conversions and restoration projects such as the repairs to York Minster after the fire in 1984, and the rebuilding of the ancient hammer-beam roof of the Great Hall of Stirling Castle in 1997. The largely one-off nature of such building projects provided the ideal market for the small parcels of well-grown estate oak that could still be found.

Yet, overall, we must picture the domestic hardwood industry today as one only just clinging on. After the clear-up of the Great Storm, it experienced a rapid decline, and today it utilises only a small fraction of the home-grown timber volume it handled in the lean post-war years. The sought-after furniture and veneer markets require trees that are the end product of properly managed woodlands, which now, as far as hardwoods are concerned, are in decline. But the home industry will survive in a small way for a long time to come as private estates eke out their timber resources and as the occasional 'prime cuts' are salvaged from the ageing broadleaves resource in the wider countryside and the 'fallers' in winter gales.

For many people, if not for the timber trade, there is a distinctly brighter side to the 'broadleaves' picture. Broadleaves are seen more and more today as a threatened scenic resource and symbol of the countryside, and their planting, as we shall see in the next chapter, has increased. But will the modern plantings be tended and managed as they need to be if timber is ever to be produced? The promise is there, but the jury on their future is very much out.

The Softwood Industry

The contrast with the softwood industry could hardly be greater. The economic value of softwoods as a timber crop is greater than that of hardwoods because of the rapid growth of the trees, and because they are cheaper and easier to harvest. In the interwar years, the softwood industry suffered along with hardwood, but it had good reason for cheer after the Second World War. As more than nine-tenths of the consumption of timber and wood products in Britain is from conifers, the development of the softwood resource in the post-war years promised to be a fine commercial opportunity.

In 1947, the Attlee government nationalised the two industries that had used the greatest amounts of home-grown timber since Victorian times: coal mining and the railways. These markets provided huge and steady outlets, particularly for softwoods, with the big advantage that they were not markets favoured by importers. Nationalisation of these industries seemed attractive to the merchants; it offered the promise of bulk contracts and greater continuity of business than had been possible when working with the individual railway and mining companies that had existed before.

But the longer-term prospects for these markets were problematic. The mining industry had been in retreat since domestic consumption of coal switched to electricity and gas after the 1920s, and the demand for pit props declined as the industry gradually evolved from underground working to open cast after the Second World War. The railway boom was over too. Wooden railway wagons were replaced by steel, and wooden sleepers by concrete, while, in the early 1960s, Dr Beeching had added his flourish to the falling consumption of railway materials.

But change brings opportunity and in the 1960s the softwood industry began to take on a new shape. Capital investment on a large scale was needed to process the increasing supplies of timber, but investors were unwilling to make commitments without the surety of a consistent and reliable wood supply. The industry's experience of raw material purchase had not been a good one, being characterised by opportunist buying of trees from forest owners when prices were high and a metaphorical drought when they were low. The Forestry Commission's plan was to use its timber sales policy to stimulate investment. Its expanding supply of timber would be offered for sale on a planned twenty-year time horizon at a price that was pegged to the competition – imported wood. Thus, contracts would be linked to world prices. 'Small roundwood' users, like paper mills, would be offered long-term contracts to supply a proportion of their needs. This meant that the requirements of the mill could be integrated with the management of the surrounding forests.

Small roundwood, as the name suggests, comes from thinnings and from the tops of felled trees. It is used for producing pulp and paper, and for making the ubiquitous wood panels we see in DIY shops. Factories for making such wood products have to be on a very large scale to be economic. In the 1950s and '60s, the economy had started to recover from its wartime malaise, and firms were looking to start new ventures. In 1955, Airscrew Weyroc saw an opportunity when it opened a factory for making chipboard in the small town of Annan in Dumfriesshire (1955). Other new mills followed at Fort William in the west of Scotland (1966); at Workington in Cumbria (1967); and at Sudbrook in Monmouthshire (1969).

It was perhaps the Fort William pulp mill that most caught the mood of the moment. Symbolically, this was a real prize for the politicians, delivering to the people of the Highlands everything that Lovat had promised in 1919. If the challenge of arresting rural depopulation could be met successfully in the Highlands, it would be an endorsement of forestry policy throughout Britain. When Lord Polwarth, Chairman of the Scottish Council for Development and Industry, cut the first sod for the factory near the small village of Corpach, he expressed confidence that 'for the first time in 250 years, we will see repopulation and not depopulation in the Highlands'. The site selected for the plant was large enough to accommodate a hoped-for second production line, planned for 1970. Seven hundred people were employed in the plant, and nearly a thousand in the surrounding forests producing pulpwood. The project included a new quay at the foot of the

Caledonian Canal to receive shiploads of timber from home and abroad. New schools were built along with 450 new houses.[41]

Unfortunately for Fort William, the good times did not last. In the late 1970s, it was announced that the mill would close. An uncompetitive pound made it cheaper to import the manufactured pulp that was needed for making paper rather than to produce it in Britain. The situation had been made worse by a pulping technology that had rapidly become obsolete and too expensive to run. The mill, of course, was not alone in its economic misfortune; the recession of the late 1970s forced large parts of the wood-processing industry (and industry generally in Britain) to close down.

Coals to Newcastle

While we may admire the manual skills of the nineteenth-century wood-workers referred to earlier in this book, the mechanical skills of the twentieth century are in their own way just as impressive, and not easily replaced. To the foresters in 1980 the closures were a bitter blow. Not only did they mean a loss of income, a temporary situation perhaps, but, worse, the permanent loss of much human expertise. Fortunately the losses were forestalled from an unexpected quarter: Sweden wanted to buy wood. The quaysides of the ports of Montrose, Inverness, Shoreham, Ipswich and the Tyne were suddenly full of seemingly endless stacks of pulpwood waiting to cross the North Sea. Suffering from depressed wood prices at home, Swedish forest owners stopped selling pulpwood to their giant pulp mills. The lifeline was gratefully grasped by Forest Thinnings, a subsidiary of the Economic Forestry Group, which started a rush of forestry companies to export Britain's unwanted pulpwood.

After its setbacks, the forestry industry started afresh in the 1980s. By 1982 the pound had settled to a new, more competitive level. Britain found itself with an expanding and uncommitted supply of timber to offer to prospective investors. What happened next was neatly summarised in an article by Barry Gamble and Simon Verdon in the journal *Accountancy*:

> If we in this country have any difficulty in sorting out the importance of our forestry sector, then overseas investors would appear to have fewer difficulties in appreciating the picture. Since 1983, following the recession in the late 1970s, over £650 million on new investment in this sector and a further

£400 million in planned expansion of capacity, has brought to the UK some of the most advanced timber processing technology available. The investment funds for this expansion have come from the US, Canada, Germany and Scandinavia.[42]

Men or Machines?

Where innovation in the timber markets changed the complexion of the wood-processing sector in the post-war years, mechanisation revolutionised work in the forest. The chainsaw gets a thoroughly bad press, but tree surgery, forestry, farming and even the ambitious gardener today would not be the same without the labour-saving benefits of this universal device. Danarm was the first company to introduce a one-man chainsaw after the Second World War, but it was heavy and cumbersome to use. By the 1960s, saws were smaller, lighter and more portable, and were readily taken up as the everyday tool of the tree feller. A large tree that would have taken two men an hour to fell with a cross-cut saw could be felled in five minutes with a one-man power saw. The pace of mechanisation varied from place to place, with lowland situations first, upland later. By the 1970s, a range of more specialised forest equipment had come into general use. Purpose-built forest machines for extracting timber had supplanted the modified farm tractors that had come into use, and the use of horses had been phased out almost completely.

From an industrial point of view, mechanisation is a wonderful thing, doing away with the drudgery of hand labour and providing a safer working environment. But there is a social price to pay for the economic gain. While forestry employers in the 1960s and '70s sought efficiency, they were at the same time failing to provide the long-term substitute for a declining farming industry that people had hoped for. Unhappy though this episode was, hindsight suggests that the decline of forestry workers in the more populous parts of the post-war countryside was swallowed up by the rapid change in its social structure, a process that the social historian Howard Newby saw as the 'Eclipse of the Rural World'.[43] But in the more remote communities where change is slow and every single job was valued, the loss of forest jobs was hard felt, and in the remote corners of Galloway and the Highlands of Scotland, it still rankles even today.

Sweden, in the 1980s, became the dominant force in forest machinery, exporting to the world well-known brands like Husqvarna and state-of-the-art cross-country vehicles for extracting timber to the roadside, where it could be picked up by a lorry. Modern chainsaws, for all their labour-saving benefits, still mean hard manual work for professional woodcutters, and sprains and back injuries lead to absenteeism or, worse, permanent injury. When, in the 1970s, forestry workers started to complain about 'vibration white finger' – a complaint brought on by the use of vibrating tools such as chainsaws – it was time to find a better way. The harvester made its first appearance in the 1980s. This sophisticated machine could almost do it all: cut down the trees, strip off the branches, saw them up and stack the wood and timber ready for the sawmill (see Picture 15).

Sawmilling had fared rather better in the recession of the late 1970s than the small roundwood industry, helped, it seems, by the Forestry Commission which continued to support its customers through the recession. Whether the shake-out of businesses in a recession is viewed as good news or bad depends on where you sit, but the failure of the weaker companies and the consolidation of the survivors put the collective industry into a stronger position to face a demanding future. Mergers in the 1980s led to the formation of the largest sawmilling concern in Britain, the company BSW. Created from the amalgamation of Brownlie, Smiths and Western Softwoods, it was large enough to pull its weight against the biggest sawmills in Europe.

Markets never stand still. By the 1990s sawmillers knew they would have to raise their game to win a share of the large and demanding market for constructional timber – house-building – which had traditionally been dominated by imports. Investment in drying kilns, 'finishing' equipment and the production of 'engineered' timber products helped to add value and gain a wider acceptance for British timber in the market. Timber supply from forests would continue to increase as the forests planted in the post-war boom reached maturity. Just one cloud was on the horizon. The trade found itself in a swirl of controversy over the environmental credibility of timber.

The Forest Industry and Environmentalism

It says something about the pick-up of environmental problems that it is only in the late 1980s that we come to one of the great issues of the moment: timber, forests and the environment. Forests worldwide are near the top of the environmental worry list that has progressed beyond the agitation of environmentalists to become a matter of keen concern to governments and international agencies like the United Nations. The gathering awareness of the role that trees and forests play in the global climate might have passed the *home* timber trade by, had it not been for the part played by the importers in bringing in timber from East Asia, Africa and, most of all, from the Amazon basin where tree felling was (and still is) leading to deforestation on a huge and life-threatening scale.

Suddenly, in the 1980s, timber was pictured as the villain. Pictures of burnt-out or logged forests were shown to the public in magazines and on television. Questions were asked about the source of the timber products being sold and whether they came from well-managed forests. Passions also ran high in the United States where concerns about the logging industry and its threat to 'old growth' areas burst into the open. The northern spotted owl, an endangered species, was adopted by environmentalists as the symbol of the ancient 'primary' forest found in the untouched wilderness areas of the Pacific North-west. Thousands of jobs in that region depended on the economy of the timber industry. Protestors chained themselves to trees as the lumber companies advanced into new areas.

In the late 1980s, the World Wildlife Fund (later the World Wide Fund for Nature) proposed a system of 'green' labelling for timber. Its advertised aim was to limit international trade to timber that came from environmentally sound sources and to do this by voluntary means through mobilising the purchasing power of timber consumers. The proposal was that forests would be 'certified' against a list of 'indicative criteria' of good forest management, and that the timber produced from them would then be subject to a documented 'chain of custody'. The criteria were to be drawn up by people 'independent of government', including a 'balanced representation from the forestry and environmental community'.[44] It further proposed the setting up of the Forestry Stewardship Council (FSC) to administer the scheme. The FSC promoted their label as a means of ensuring 'environmentally appropriate, socially beneficial, and economically viable management of the world's forests'. In Britain, the FSC established itself as the front-runner among a number of proposed timber-labelling schemes. The crunch for the timber trade came when public authorities announced that they would only commission building work that used timber from certified sources and when a retailers' group (the WWF 95 Plus group) committed itself to selling only wood products with an FSC label.

What did the timber merchants make of this fast developing situation? They thought that the benefits of growing and marketing a renewable resource ought to be obvious and that the industry was being unfairly attacked. 'It has to be appreciated that certification is primarily a solution to problems faced, not in the UK, but elsewhere', said Martin Mathers of the WWF in 1994.[45] According to the United Nations, 70 per cent of tropical forest clearance was for ranching, settlement and supplying local populations with their wood needs, so where, the timber trade asked, was the justification for interfering with trade?[46]

But for all the irritation that the timber trade felt at what they saw as interference, they were drawn into the process. The system would answer the challenges facing the credibility of their product in the marketplace. For the home producers, the status of home-grown 'certified' timber as an independently assured, sustainable and 'eco-friendly' raw material meant it could be promoted for its unique qualities against other materials used in the building industry, such as (energy-intensive) concrete and steel. With the passage of time, the concept of certification gained momentum. Merchants and contractors in Britain contributed to a 'certification standard' which was launched publicly in London in June 1999.[47]

How effective was certification in addressing the problem for which it was intended? Did it put the management of the tropical forests on a sustainable basis and close down illegal logging? Today it can best be described as work in progress. Twenty-five per cent of the world's industrial harvest of wood is said to be certified, including about 70 per cent of the area of 'commercial' woodland in Britain.[48] But claims of illegal and unsustainable logging practice in the Third World seem to come as thick and fast as ever.

9

NEW DIRECTIONS

I f productivity and efficiency were the standards by which land use in
Britain is judged, the development of forestry in the post-war years
was a success story and its contribution to the economy is now far
greater than it was in 1945. In the shadow of the Second World War the
drive to use every acre of land for the production of food or timber was
seldom questioned. But, as earlier chapters have shown, there was increasing unease about the way forest policy focused on timber production and
its effects on the landscape. In part at least, this point of view was sympto-
matic of a fast-changing social environment in which an appreciation of
the aesthetic and recreational values of the countryside came into much
greater prominence. In the 1980s this trend culminated in a historic change
of emphasis in forest policy.

The single issue that stood out most in the kaleidoscope of countryside
politics in the 1980s was the reform of agriculture. Food surpluses in the
countries of the EEC were thought to be getting out of hand and it was
believed that considerable areas of land would have to be taken out of production. Pundits talked of a possible surplus of 3 million hectares in Britain
by 2000. The Agriculture Bill, before Parliament in 1985, ended the post-war
era of unqualified support for farming and gave the government agriculture
departments a responsibility to promote conservation. In the spirit of farm
reform, land was set aside and the first wave of agri-environment schemes
was launched to a rather bemused agriculture industry.

One element of the new approach was the Farm Woodland Scheme. This
was real innovation when it was introduced in 1988 because agricultural
policy had not previously encouraged farmers to plant trees. The main aim

of the scheme was 'to promote diversification on farms so that farmers [were] better able to cope with the consequence of CAP reform'. The idea of encouraging tree planting on lowland farms rather than in the uplands was widely supported since, unlike food crops, timber was not in surplus and it was thought that many farmed landscapes could benefit from more tree cover. Lord Strathclyde, a government minister and spokesman on forestry, reinforced the political message in a speech in 1991: 'What is happening is that forestry is emerging from its strongholds in the hills where it was driven by the priority given in the past to agriculture ... to offer a much wider range of forests and woodlands, and a much wider range of public benefits.'[1]

The social evolution in the 1960s and '70s was illustrated by a wave of public interest in the environment, marked by a rapid growth in the membership of the voluntary environmental bodies. The combined memberships of the larger conservation societies (such as the National Trust and the RSPB) increased from around half a million in 1970 to nearly 5 million at the turn of the century. Whereas the public at large had had little interest or involvement in the land economy during the early post-war years, joining one or more of the voluntary bodies provided people with real insights into the workings of the countryside and the opportunity to join forces with others of like mind in campaigns or fund-raising for worthy causes.

Land in Trust

A manifestation of this growth in the voluntary sector was the acquisition of woodland by trusts, societies and associations. The National Trust is perhaps the most obvious body to mention here and of course it was the first in the field when it was founded in the late nineteenth century. By the 1960s, it had built up a significant woodland landholding through the gift or purchase of interesting scenic woods and by acquiring woodland as part and parcel of its numerous estate properties. On a similar scale, the county wildlife trust movement acquired many woods, concentrating in their case on semi-natural sites rather than on planted estate woods. Collectively, the wildlife trusts enjoyed a rapid growth in the 1960s and '70s. The ownership and direct management of the trusts' many wildlife sites was their main *raison d'être* and what most attracted the knowledgeable amateur naturalists that formed the core of their memberships. Landownership provided the trusts with the opportunity to pursue their charitable objectives in an active and practical way, and to develop new skills in conservation management. Having removed any threats to the main wildlife interest on their sites, the trusts appointed wardens and designated the areas as local wildlife reserves with either restricted or open access to the public.

The Woodland Trust's founding in 1972 was another example of this trend. Having grown to become today's largest woodland conservation charity in the UK, its development is of particular interest. The Trust was founded as an off-shoot of the Devon Wildlife Trust, with the aim of protecting the small woods and copses that other organisations would not take on.

Kenneth Watkins, its founder and leading light for many years, was a retired businessman and prize-winning amateur wildlife cameraman who, as a trustee of the Devon Naturalist Trust, had given himself the task of searching out and acquiring new nature reserves for that body. The story goes that he embarrassed his fellow trustees with just one too many woodland sites for purchase at a time when the Trust was trying to diversify the range of its nature reserves. The Trust's response to him was to suggest that he set up a separate trust specifically for woods. Its first purchases were the Avon Valley Woods near Kingsbridge in South Devon. From these small beginnings in the West Country, the Trust became the owner of over 1,000 woods throughout the UK. Its remarkable membership increase in recent years – up from 80,000 in 2000 to 200,000 in 2010 – is evidence indeed of the public's increasing interest in the whole field of tree conservation.

Alongside the voluntary bodies' enthusiasm for the purchase of sites of existing wildlife interest, a completely new trend in charity landownership began to take shape in the late 1980s. The creation or recreation of freshwater habitats, bogs and heaths, and the planting of native woodland on former agricultural land, became the new frontier for some of the better-funded charities. By taking advantage of the loosening grip of the farming industry on its land base, the aim was to return the land to something approaching its pre-agricultural natural state.

Deep pockets were required for the purchase of agricultural land and fortunately the arrival on the scene of a range of new funding sources in the 1990s provided a boost to the new trend. The launch of the government's National Lottery in 1994 was a particularly decisive moment since the considerable resources it provided made all the difference between the adoption and the rejection of project ideas. With very little ceremony, large sums of money were granted for woodland projects. In 1996 the Heritage Lottery Fund grant-aided the Woodland Trust's purchase of the sheep farm of Glen Finglas in the Trossachs and, in the same year, the Royal Scottish Forestry Society's purchase of Cashel Farm on Loch Lomondside, with grants of £1.4 million[2] and £800,000[3] respectively. For some types of woodland work in the 1990s, the voluntary bodies found themselves almost awash with money as the lottery boards were looking for willing partners who could rapidly turn cash into delivered projects on the ground. One of the Millennium Commission's tree projects, the Woodland Trust's 'Woods on Your Doorstep', alone attracted a grant of £10.5 million[4] and the Scottish Millennium Forest was given another £11.34 million.[5] Another new source of funding for trees was the landfill tax. Local authorities in 1996 were given powers to collect taxes from the operators of landfill sites to discourage the depositing of biodegradable waste and to distribute the money to green projects – the first example of green taxes used to benefit woodland conservation.

Nor was the 'grant' funding for woodlands entirely confined to public sector sources. Private companies saw the advantage of an association with tree interests, either as a way of providing community benefits in their local areas or as a means of projecting a green image to their customers and a wider audience. BP, currently the villain of the piece in the Gulf of Mexico, was one of the foremost examples. In 2003, the company, with its large refinery in Grangemouth on the Firth of Forth, pledged to give £10 million for a ten-year programme 'aiming to create 10,000 hectares of new woodland' in Scotland;[6] a fund that was distributed to several projects.

The Broadleaves Review

What had prepared the way for this new and promising funding outlook? Since the 1970s, environmentalists had been looking for a signal from the government that its forest policy would be broadened beyond its focus on the production of timber. Periods of rapid evolution in thinking are often remembered through a single transforming event or turning point – a sort of eureka moment that became a trigger for change. *Broadleaves in Britain* – a consultative paper published in 1984[7] – sought opinions on what should be done to encourage 'positive and sympathetic' management of the country's broadleaved woods.

An accumulation of pressures had prompted the review. Dutch elm disease had decimated the English elms in the 1970s, while 'advances' in agriculture threatened hedgerows everywhere and were leaving parts of Britain in an almost prairie-like condition. Then there was the issue of ancient woodlands. The difficulty was that ancient woods were not identified on the ground, nor – apart from those designated as SSSI – were they regarded as nature reserves in a way that would qualify them for legal protection. The case for their special status had, however, been succinctly made by a House of Lords committee that recommended that woods of 'very special interest to nature conservation or of particular historical importance' should be managed as nature reserves where 'any sale of wood that happened to be profitable would be purely incidental'.[8]

The question then, in the metaphorical small print of the review, was a forest policy issue of fundamental importance for the future: should the production of timber still be the dominant theme of forest policy? Or should it be enlarged to embrace a fully multi-purpose philosophy in which environmental and social benefits would sit equally beside timber production as an objective?

There was really only one answer to the question. In a clear shift of public opinion, there were new expectations. Forests should be managed for a wider variety of purposes, and forest management should become a more participative process. Particularly significant was the 1985 Wildlife and Countryside Act which gave the Forestry Commission a duty to balance timber production with environmental benefits. It became commonplace for voluntary bodies to be represented on the advisory panels that affected their interests and to be consulted over grant decisions. Tree planting became subject to a plethora of new 'processes' aiming to achieve what the politicians like to call 'getting the right trees in the right places'. 'Indicative strategies', integrated forest design plans and environmental assessment for tree planting entered the dictionary of government forest policy, while conservation policies were adopted for ancient woods.

The 1992 Earth Conference

Even though the pressures on ancient woodland in Britain were only a pinprick in comparison with the destruction of tropical rain forests, the principle was in some ways the same. At a star-studded gathering of politicians from around the world, the Earth conference in Rio de Janeiro in 1992 was the first time that forests had figured at the top table of international affairs. The part played by forests in regulating the carbon cycle of the atmosphere and the truly global threats to the environment posed by carbon emissions had pushed forests into the limelight. This was the moment when the idea that countries should reduce emissions was officially launched. Perhaps it was too much to ask that there should be easy agreement on what was at first proposed – a Forests Convention that would have imposed a break on the economic advancement of the developing countries. 'Environment versus development' viewpoints from different parts of the world were aired at Rio in an acrimonious debate.

Rio, however, did produce a great deal more than most people had expected. Standing alongside the Climate and Biodiversity Conventions, for which the conference is best known, was a voluntary statement of 'forest principles', subsequently adopted in Europe and around the world. This introduced the concept of 'sustainable forest management' and the notion that all the outputs of the forests, environmental and social, as well as economic, should be considered and planned for together. The practice of sustainable forest management became the 'gold standard' of forestry, since recognised in government 'forestry standards' and in the independently assured 'certification standard'.

Rebuilding Biodiversity

Nothing epitomised the new directions in forestry in Britain in the late 1980s more than the change from commercial forestry in the uplands to afforestation with 'new native woods'. Some of the new woods were on former agricultural sites in the lowlands and others on exactly the same upland sheep grazings that had previously been sought after by foresters for timber production. Conifer planting went into a steep decline, while broadleaved planting surged from less than 1,000 hectares annually in 1985 to 10,500 hectares by 2000.

The whole idea of 'new native woods' seems, if taken literally, a contradiction in terms. For some tree planters, it simply meant planting native species on the lines of traditional forestry patterns. For others, it meant using mixtures of trees planted in ways that emulated the more random patterns found in nature. More open space was incorporated, shrub species were introduced as well as large forest trees, and preference was given to the use of local tree seed sources over more distant ones. To achieve a more uneven and 'natural' appearance, any ground preparation needed was carried out with minimum disturbance. Natural regeneration rather than planting was favoured where there were mother trees in the vicinity to provide a scatter of seed.

What had prompted this change from commercial woodland to new native woods? The fashionable search for 'diversification' of farmland and the rejection by some people of commercial motivations for forestry are the obvious and immediate answers to this question. Public opinion surveys consistently put wildlife at the top of the reasons for expanding forest cover and ecologists argued that there were many strong ecological reasons for planting more and larger native woods.[9] For many people, supporting the creation of new native woods in Britain seemed the least they could do in the face of declining biodiversity and worldwide concerns about the loss of tropical forests.

Is it too fanciful to suggest that a major stimulant to the creation of new woods was the burgeoning interest in ancient woods? The place of ancient woods in a book about forest and woodland expansion is, in a way, in the background, but overshadows much of the work of planting new woods. While new woods will never be ancient woods, conservation bodies made much of the emotional connections between the two and no appeal for funding new woods was complete without an almost copybook reference to saving ancient woodland.

Yet there is also a real point of contact. The ideas of 'landscape working' and 'woodland habitat networks' began to take hold in the late 1990s.[10] The thinking was that new woods could be planted to 'buffer and link' the scattered fragments of ancient woodland. The networks could serve two objectives. They could provide protection from unwanted influences from nearby land (such as chemical sprays on adjoining arable fields), and perhaps even provide migration routes for plant and animals in the face of climate change.

Scotland led the way with some truly massive woodland restoration schemes – conservation projects that inspired a level of investment from landowners and funding bodies on a hitherto unimagined scale. Scotland has the advantage over other parts of Britain in having large traditional landownerships – former sheep farms and deer forests – which provided the scale of activity needed for really effective restoration ecology. As well as the advantage of size, their existing semi-natural character provided a head start towards greater 'naturalisation'. The Cannich area of Inverness-shire –

a region of relict pine and birch woods set in spectacular Highland scenery – was chosen for just these characteristics, with the added advantage that it is largely devoid of settlement. Over 19,000 hectares of land is now in the three main conservation ownerships that form the centrepiece of the project.[11] Some conservationists even predict the reintroduction, in time, of the bear and wolf!

Another large-scale woodland restoration project in Scotland was triggered by a sequence of events no one had predicted or planned for; a lesson perhaps that land-use change can come, not from the interplay of market factors, but from an entirely unexpected direction. In the 1990s the city of Glasgow had a water quality problem which was traced back to the possibility of cryptosporidium pollution originating in Loch Katrine, a large reservoir that is the primary water supply for the city and its surroundings. The surrounds of the loch had been described as the biggest sheep farm in Scotland, with a flock of 17,000 sheep. However, sheep and clean water supplies can be a bad mix and after this incident it was decided to move the sheep. Together with adjoining properties in like-minded conservation ownership, Loch Katrine and its surroundings became part of a 21,000-hectare project[12] described as 'the largest woodland and habitat landscape restoration project ever carried out in the UK'.[13] The scheme will restore woodland, wildlife and clean water to the now more confident water-drinking public in Glasgow.

Conservation interests in England and Wales have no such open-space advantages and must struggle instead with smaller areas and highly priced land. In contrast to the upland examples from Scotland, lowland farms offered little scope for woodland creation beyond the boundaries of a single farm running to a hundred hectares or so, sometimes more. This is one area in which the Woodland Trust excelled, when most potential tree planters were frightened off by expensive land. Determined fund-raising produced impressive results; twenty-one acquisitions had been made in the National Forest (see below) by 2005 and, riding the crest of the wave, farms and small estates were acquired for tree planting in key conservation areas from Cornwall to County Durham, and from Monmouthshire to Essex.[14] People were happy to contribute to tree planting far away from where they lived, which they would probably never see.

One of the most innovative ways of raising funds for woodland planting is through 'carbon offset' schemes, which depend on the way trees 'sequester' and fix carbon from the atmosphere through photosynthesis. Commercial concerns and voluntary bodies offered tree-planting services to individuals and companies wishing to offset their personal carbon 'footprint' or that of their business activities. 'Carbon calculators' enable people to work out the carbon emissions associated with their lifestyle or with specific activities such as air travel, with a view to paying a fee to offset it, possibly to be used for tree planting. Such schemes are not, however, without their critics in the environmental movement. Some people see the promotion of tree planting for carbon storage as an unwelcome distraction from the real challenge of persuading industry to move into low-carbon technologies; buying its way out of trouble, as it were, by tree planting. Others counter that such criticisms ignore the multiple benefits of well-sited tree planting. 'We believe that tree planting [for carbon lock-up] can only support wider programmes of action and should never be used in isolation', says the Woodland Trust in its *Carbon-plus* brochure. By 2007, the sale of such services provided a valuable stream of income for tree planting in Britain, said to have increased from £20 million in 2005 to £60 million in 2007.[15]

Can planting trees really help to save the planet? Nobody claims that planted forests can restore the rich natural biodiversity of the original primary forests of the world, but could they at least help to reduce the build-up of carbon in the atmosphere or, through timber production, divert some of the pressures for deforestation? It has been argued that small-scale tree planting is whistling in the wind where the great environmental problems of the day are concerned, and cannot register even on a microscopic scale. The bald arithmetic of this must be true. But the same might be said of many other human actions to improve the world we live in. Action has to start somewhere; people need to be doing something as individuals when the big battalions – the international agencies – seem helpless to act.

Woods and Farmers

We jump now from the creation of new native woodland to the planting of new woods on farms. It was not perhaps the best start for the Farm Woodland Scheme (FWS) that its conception was more about the surplus of agricultural land than any real strategy for agriculture, or for woodland. There are nearly 60,000 existing small woods less than 10 hectares in size in Britain, many of them on farms and many neglected. But it was in the nature of the FWS (and the Farm Woodland Premium Scheme (FWPS) that replaced it in 1992) that it would be about creating new woods rather than bringing existing ones into management.

This unwelcoming analysis, however, would be to dismiss the FWS too quickly. It was plainly asking too much of the scheme that it would imbue British farmers overnight with a culture of farm forestry. Nevertheless, anything that increased their interest in woods would be beneficial, and the many hundreds of new woods created under the schemes will indeed 'enhance the landscape, encourage wildlife and get farmers more interested in timber production' if they are maintained and looked after. A novel element was that farmers, as well as an up-front grant (through the Forestry Commission's Woodland Grant Scheme), were offered a series of annual payments (for twenty years for conifers, thirty years for mixed broadleaves and forty years for oak and beech) to compensate them for the agricultural support that they would lose by tree planting.

In England, tree planting in the farmed landscape was enthusiastically championed by the Countryside Commission which produced a series of woodland policy statements in the 1980s and '90s, and in 1985 floated ideas for a series of community forests and the creation of a completely new 'National Forest'. It also grant-aided small-scale landscape plantings and gave 'pump-priming' finance to not-for-profit bodies like the National Small Woods Association and (before its functions were divided) Coed Cymru, a body devoted to promoting the economic viability of broad-leaved woodlands in Wales and the use of Welsh timber.

The site for the National Forest – selected by the Commission after consideration of five possible locations – covers the mainly farmed landscape between the cities of Birmingham, Derby and Leicester, and includes the defunct South Leicestershire coalfield, altogether an area of 200 square miles. Marketing, finance and public relations were led by a government-owned National Forest Company, whose strategy was to 'create and demonstrate a modern, multi-purpose forest [to] contain working woodlands contributing to supplies of home-grown timber, provide new opportunities for recreation, create new wildlife habitats and offer new uses of farmland and help to stimulate the region's economy'.

As well as the ordinary forest and farm grants, tree planters in the National Forest benefited from an additional top-up grant known as the Forest Tender Scheme, a clever device designed to distribute a pot of extra government money through a process of competitive bidding. Grants were awarded on a points system for woodland planting and related environmental amenities for the public, such as walking routes, horse trails, ponds and other wildlife sites. When it became obvious that the easy 'hits' for tree planting had been realised, the company was given powers to buy and own its own land. This meant it could respond more spontaneously to properties offered for sale on the open market and at the same time get the chance to restructure farms to the advantage of the forest.

Politicians love a success story and, looking back on the early years of the National Forest, one of the striking things that put it on the map was the frequency of visits it received from senior government ministers. Political interest in woodland affairs was always welcome but, at a time of great innovation in woods and tree-related issues, it was a shame that the interest was not more widely shared among other forest initiatives with an equally challenging, interesting and beneficial role to play in the nation's affairs. But the National Forest today stands as an example of the speed at which, given a fair wind from government and generous funding, land can be transformed from lowland farming into farm and community woods. Set against the ultimate goal of creating a wooded landscape extending to around one-third of the project area, the forest had covered 18 per cent of the area by 2008, compared with 6 per cent at its formal 'founding' in 1995; a striking achievement in the face of a ferocious determination by most landowners and farmers to hold on to their every acre for farming. This was already a change sufficient to make a real difference to local people. Asked in 2006 whether such rapid afforestation to the ultimate target of one-third of forest cover might alienate local communities, Sophie Churchill (currently Chief Executive) thought not; it would instead build 'civic pride, community identity and economic resilience'.[16]

Between Town and Country – Trees on the Urban Fringe

In contrast to the setting up of the National Forest in 1995, there was no big show about the development of the Midland Reafforesting Association in 1903, an initiative that reminds us today that everything really has been tried before! *The Times* in 1912 described the Midland Reafforesting Association as the only society in Britain that aimed at 'spreading information and existing interest concerning forestry amongst the general public'.[17] The association had the formal constitution of a Friendly Society and raised money by public subscription. Its aim was to 'green' sites of industrial dereliction in the Black Country, where great swathes of abandoned land had resulted from industrial contraction in the second half of the nineteenth century. It was said that there were 30,000 acres of land just 'used for piling rubbish upon'.[18]

A typical tree-planting site was one of pit and furnace waste in the grounds of an isolation hospital at Moorcroft, near Moxley, where in 1905 the association planted 31 acres with 60,000 alder, wych elm, ash, sycamore and willow. It also had a social purpose, organising school events such as an annual Arbor Day Festival – a fashionable idea of its time, with origins in 1870s Nebraska in the United States, where it is still today a national holiday. Young lives experienced a great day on 17 December 1907 when Arbor Day in the Black Country involved 105 children from ten different schools. Talks on tree planting and practical instruction were given to the children.

Were it still in existence today, the association would have a good claim to have been the first body to tackle tree planting on what are the most difficult woodland creation projects of all: ex-industrial and mineral sites. The problems it encountered were typical of those that dogged planting on such sites throughout the twentieth century. They included the 'hope' value connected with mineral-rich deposits, lack of planning controls on mineral sites which meant that operators could abandon them without reinstating the ground to productive use, as well as fires and vandalism to its planted woods. Nor did it help that the prevailing idea was that all forestry should be 'commercial' when the need was clearly for something different. The association survived for twenty years but closed down after the First World War with only a small fraction of its planting ambitions realised.

Much time passed before there was the political will to tackle these problems. John Barr's *Derelict Britain*[19] was a hard-hitting exposure of the 'national scandal' of derelict and industrial wasteland, written in the immediate aftermath of the 1966 tragedy at Aberfan at Merthyr Tydfil. Barr estimated that there were 250,000 'squandered' acres of derelict land in Britain, nearly all of it 'bang in the middle of intensively populated areas'. Aberfan focused public attention on the problem as nothing else could have done. In the 1970s the government of the day and the development agencies turned their attention to dealing with the Swansea valley (which Barr had highlighted) and the many other blighted areas in Britain, such as south-east Wales, the Black Country, Lancashire, Durham, Northumberland and the central belt of Scotland.

The technical problems of getting trees to grow on inhospitable former mineral sites were beginning to be solved by 1970. The late John Zehetmayr's introduction to the 1979 booklet *Tree Planting on Man-made Sites in Wales*[20] records thirty years of experimentation and small-scale tree planting to stabilise and improve spoil heaps, old quarries and abandoned mineral workings. His experiments showed, for instance, that some tree species could grow perfectly well on untreated ground surfaces without the need for topsoil. And there was an unlikely spin-off from this research into man-made and disturbed soils. In the 1960s and '70s, Britain's new great motorway network emerged as a beneficiary. How would the motorways look without their tens of thousands of acres of enveloping woodland? For all the frustrations of motor travel, there can be few situations where the calming green surroundings of planted trees contribute more to the collective good of human health and welfare as they do on the verges, cuttings and embankments of these great roads (see Picture 21).

Thus, by the 1970s, some of the tools for creating what we nowadays refer to as 'urban fringe' forestry were falling into place. Central to the whole idea was the planting of vacant industrial land and the greening of transport corridors. We can readily attribute the thinking behind it to Nan Fairbrother, writing in 1970. As a landscape architect, she was interested in the relationship between the towns and cities, and the farmed countryside beyond. She proposed the development of an urban fringe that would reconcile the needs of the people in the towns and cities with the preservation of the agricultural economy outside them, commenting that we:

> should surround our towns and cities with trees. Thousands upon thousands of trees to frame our urban areas in belts of woodland and insulate their urban landscapes in the rural countryside ... One of the few advantages of our extravagant pre-planning land use is the amount of land not used at all, but wasted. If we take a large-scale map of the edge of almost any built-up area and go over the actual ground, colouring red on the map every patch of land not positively used, we finish up with a surprisingly red-spotted sheet. By planting areas of otherwise unused land we could travel into our cities through wooded landscape.[21]

What, today, do we mean by the urban fringe? Neither wholly rural nor entirely urban in its character, the urban fringe is characterised by housing developments, industrial estates, science parks, hospitals, supermarkets and by-passes. It is often a place of conflict between farmers and urban interests because of the pressure for recreational access and the threat of anti-social activity like car dumping (see Picture 33).

With the widening of forest policy in the late 1980s, the first in a new wave of urban fringe initiatives was the Black Country Forest (and the Black Country Urban Forestry Unit) which was almost, it seemed, a re-incarnation of the Midlands Reafforesting Association, but this time with the more promising background of sponsorship by a government depart-ment, the Department of Environment. As well as the planting of derelict and underdeveloped land, the Black Country Forest concept embraced the planting of trees in streets and parks and the creation of new areas of green space. The idea was that 'partner' organisations – local government, private industry and charitable trusts – would carry out the physical work of tree planting and subsequent care. By 2000, thirty-nine urban fringe tree initiatives throughout the country were being listed in a report for the Countryside Agency,[22] most of them started or supported by government agencies in a sector of urban planning that was unattractive to private land-owners and voluntary bodies alike.

High on the Countryside Agency's list were twelve new 'community for-ests' in areas of low tree cover in the hinterland of some of the great cities in England. The Red Rose Forest, for instance, started up in 1991, stretches to the north and west of Manchester and has nearly 5 million people living within 20km of the forest boundary (see Picture 26). Perhaps most people are more familiar with the term 'community forest' in the context of small, rural, community-inspired initiatives of the kind described later, but when applied to the urban fringe forests the name is at least aspirational, recognis-ing that it needs to be managed *with* or *by* the community and not just *for* them. To help shape the forest as a community asset, local people need to know of its existence, how to communicate with it and how to play a part in its development. Volunteer activity is encouraged to attribute a sense of community ownership. Project teams were appointed in the community forests as energisers to stimulate and lead community action, promoting the forest concept to local people and staging events to engage the interest of local and national politicians.

Above all, the urban fringe forests were well placed to engage the inter-est of children and to give them their moment with nature. Children love planting trees, and for those living in towns, and therefore unfamiliar with the countryside, the birth and life of a new tree seems particularly poignant.

According to television personality Clive Anderson, 'planting a tree is a rite of passage, something to be learned at an early age, like tying a shoelace or telling the time'.[23] Where 'school plots' had been a popular scheme in the 1950s, 'Forest School' served a similar purpose in the 1990s. Originating in Scandinavia, the scheme was introduced by a network of schools and local authorities with the aim of encouraging children to explore nature and develop practical skills in a natural setting (see Pictures 40 and 41). The Woodland Trust's 'Tree for All' initiative in 2004 promised that every child in Britain should have a chance to plant trees, and in 2007 the Welsh Assembly followed suit by instigating its 'Plant! A Tree for every Child' programme. For older people, a variation on the theme was 'green gyms' which integrate aerobic exercise with practical conservation work – an idea promoted by the British Trust for Conservation Volunteers.

It is too soon to venture a guess about the future of the new urban forests and whether they will, in the end, deliver the benefits claimed for them in the 1990s, or perhaps do even better. Will new businesses really be attracted to the greener environment that is being created and will they find employees who, with their families, want to live in the formerly blighted but now greener environments made ready for them? Will the more leafy surroundings have an impact on house prices? How is the political will, enjoyed at the outset of the project, to be sustained over the long term? It would be unrealistic to think that their grand designs will not change in the course of a typical project period of forty years, but will the change be for the good or will the project be derailed by economic cut-backs? The National Urban Forestry Unit (a development of the Black Country Urban Forestry Unit) was closed down in 2005, just as it was having a real impact beyond its home patch in the Black Country, on the pretext that it had done its work! For a concept with so much promise, not good.

Small is Beautiful – Getting Involved

So far, most of the initiatives that have been mentioned were carried out by large organisations or were part of a government-led scheme. What has not been emphasised is the groundswell of interest in tree planting and woodland conservation among individuals and small groups of people.

The concept of community woods was not a new one in the 1990s – a small amount of woodland purchase had become typical of many parish council budgets. But it enjoyed a new lease of life when it was promoted by grant-aiding bodies such as the Millennium Forest for Scotland Trust. The Trust encouraged small, mainly rural communities to submit proposals for small woods, either to rehabilitate existing woodland or to plant new ones, so encouraging a 'revival of the connection' between the community and its woodlands. In support of these aims, the Trust helped communities with 'capacity building', and successfully tutored the creation of seventy-two initiatives in remote communities. In England and Wales, the Woodland Trust's 'community forest network' was created as a self-help group and a newsletter launched to harness the collective force of volunteers and to keep them in touch with the Trust's campaigning themes. Another idea was Tree Wardens, an initiative taken in 1989 by the Tree Council. Now running in over sixty local authority areas, tree wardens are volunteers appointed by parish councils and community organisations to foster local interest in trees, watch out for threats from development and keep an eye open for opportunities for tree planting.

A plethora of regional and local 'grass-roots' campaigning charities prospered in the 1990s, some of them punching well above their weight in influence and ambitions. Reforesting Scotland, a charity founded in 1991, campaigned for a new 'forest culture' and the creation of the 'Second Great Wood of Caledon'. Highland Birchwoods gave advice on the management and use of semi-natural woodland and Trees for Life, a conservation charity based in Findhorn, Morayshire, championed the restoration of the pinewoods in Scotland and encouraged volunteer tree planting. In Wales, Coed Cymru fostered the use of local hardwoods and encouraged the management of neglected woodland.

Purchasing or owning a wood is a step too far for most people, but not for everyone. Chris Starr's *Woodland Management – A Practical Guide* devotes a whole chapter to buying and owning a wood: 'Don't expect to make money', is Starr's warning. 'For many people, the simple enjoyment of wandering through their woodland in different seasons is enough justification for owning it.'[24] He suggested that 'a small freehold woodland could just about be purchased for the price of a family motor car' (this was in 2005) and gave examples of how some small owners had fared in rehabilitating or planting attractive mixed woodlands.

Then, Now and in the Future

A hundred years ago it would have been impossible to imagine that the aristocratic monopoly of landownership would ever end. The tradition of the estate woodland, integrated as it was with farming and shooting, does have its proponents, but, as we have seen, that kind of land tenure is now greatly diminished. Tree people need not look back on this era as a golden age. It was not. Britain had reduced its forest cover nearly to the brink of extermination in the nineteenth century and, such as it was, the enjoyment of it by the public was heavily curtailed by the traditional caution of land-owners towards the whole idea of public access.

The year 1895 is generally regarded as the low point of Britain's forest cover. A census of woodlands showed that about 5 per cent of the land surface was covered with trees, spread fairly evenly between England, Scotland and Wales. Britain had arrived at a turning point and a gathering force of informed opinion thought that something should be done about it. Inevitably, this came to a head in the First World War when timber shortages became the trigger for political action to reverse the trend of forest decline.

For all the twists and turns, it is easiest to picture the reforestation of Britain in three phases. Just as Roy Robinson had predicted in 1943, the *strategic phase* that had started in 1919 turned into an *industrial phase* in the 1960s with the creation of a national investment with 'important peacetime claims on public attention'. The aim was to create a forest industry through tree planting and the development of timber processing to meet the demand for wood products at home and compete in a world market. And just as that first change was largely unremarkable and seamless, so the next change was noisy and fractious. Through an open and sometimes disputed process in the mid-to-late 1980s, there came a eureka moment: the adoption by public demand of a *multi-purpose phase* when tree planting and forest management became an activity to be undertaken for pleasure as well as for profit.

Today, forest cover in Britain is more than twice what it was in 1895: 9 per cent in England, 17 per cent in Scotland and 14 per cent in Wales. Every county and region has more woodland than it did in 1895. The 'snapshots' of forest cover for the years 1895, 1947 and 1998 that are illustrated in figure 1 show the broad pattern of increase in each county and region in Britain over the hundred-year period.[25]

The broad groupings illustrated in the figure cannot display the underly-ing detail.[26] In England, woodland cover varies from only 1.5 per cent in

Cambridgeshire (up from 1.2 per cent in 1895) to 22 per cent in Surrey. The two most wooded counties, Surrey and Sussex (with an average together of 20 per cent tree cover), can attribute their good fortune more to the historical endowment of woodland from earlier times than to twentieth-century planting. But, more generally, it is afforestation that has made the big difference and, unsurprisingly, this difference is greater in upland counties than in the lowland ones. For instance, woodland in Northumberland increased from less than 4 per cent in 1895 to 15 per cent today.

In Wales, Merioneth (now mostly within the county boundary of Gwynedd) and Glamorgan show the greatest increase in woodland cover, increasing from an average of 4 per cent in 1985 to 18 per cent today. Yet these two counties could not be more different in character – the former sparsely populated and rural in character, the latter, populous and industrial.

Scotland is the land of the greatest change, its beckoning hills the subject of much tree planting for timber between the 1960s and the 1980s, though nowadays its afforestation is more likely to be wildlife oriented. Looking at the landscape of Scotland today, it is hard to believe that in 1895 there was an average of only 4.5 per cent woodland cover. Kirkcudbrightshire (now part of Dumfries and Galloway) started with only 3.3 per cent forest in 1885 and today has 34.1 per cent. At the other extreme, planting in the agricultural counties of Scotland – the Lothians, Fife, Angus and Berwickshire – was on a small scale. Farming and farm woods were the priority here; woods and shelter belts were planted to protect crops and livestock (see Picture 22).

What of present-day woodland creation? Despite the funding innovations described in this chapter, the rate of woodland increase has declined over the past ten years. The area planted (and regenerated naturally) in 2008–9 was 6,000 hectares – a far cry from the 25,000 hectares per annum that was the average annual area planted from 1950–90. Do we actually need more trees? After a century of tree planting, have we perhaps got enough? That 'more trees' is the usual response by the public to any question about the greening of the environment is really rather an extraordinary thing.

Since the 1980s, no 'big idea' born of real necessity has come on the scene to conclusively galvanise forest policy as it did in 1919. Fairbrother's case for urban fringe planting still seems as fresh and relevant as it did forty years ago when she wrote *New Lives, New Landscapes*, but it suffers from daunting planning problems and no clearly focused champion to take it forward. Thus, urban forests always seem to be in danger of failing through the interplay of central and local government responsibilities and finance. In public opinion surveys even this worthy cause is overshadowed by interest in biodiversity and planting for wildlife. The public, constantly regaled with gloomy stories of tropical forest decline and global warming, has taken the wildlife conservation theme to its heart. But it is a long game because, apart from a few special places, the practical ability of the voluntary bodies to implement change on the landscape scale that would be required to make a difference is severely constrained by high land prices that seem to outpace inflation and make land less accessible to tree planters every year.

The coming together of environmental and timber interests implied in the last chapters of this book did not go quite as far as it might have done. After learning from the mistakes of several decades of single-minded planting for timber production in the twentieth century, it would be a shame if the message of multi-purpose forestry is not fully engaged. The formal creation of many acres of non-commercial woodland is in many ways a new phenomenon and part of the tree 'story' that is very much developing today. However, foresters make the observation that most of the woods and forests that people now enjoy and use in the countryside owe their attractive character to past or present management of timber. Woodland that is both productive and properly designed for aesthetic and human needs as well as ecological benefit would seem to 'tick the boxes'.

Will we look back on the phenomenon of climate change as a cause to which all the different tree interests can rally? Trees, it is said, are at the forefront of concerns about climate change. With their deep rooting systems and large physical presence, trees have the capacity to improve soils, ameliorate flooding, restore water tables for sustainable agriculture and provide shade and shelter for people and crops. Beyond the towns and cities, it is the fortunes of the farmers that will determine the landscape of the future and the part played by trees. Present-day dependency on cheap and unsustainable oil production and reliance upon land that can only be cropped by using chemicals and large machines is bound to change. Might trees moderate the prairie plains of East Anglia when temperature change causes desiccation and the water shortages set in? The restorative properties of trees suggest that it might be so.

Wood is necessary for civilized life, and therefore it is a basis of civilization. But wood may be regarded as merely a by-product of trees. Their greatest value is probably their beneficent effect on life, health, climate, soil, rainfall and streams. Trees beautify the country, provide shade for humans and stock, shelter crops from wind and storm and retain water in the soil at a level at which it can be used by man. The neglect of forestry in the past has accounted for the deserts that exist, because of the fact that when the tree covering disappears from the earth, the water level sinks.[27]

From *I Planted Trees* by Richard St Barbe Baker (1889–1982), founder of the society 'Men of the Trees'.

NOTES

Notes that refer to the publications that are listed in the Bibliography are referenced in abbreviated form only, thus, for instance, Chapman (1941) means D.H. Chapman's *The Seasons and the Woodman* published by Cambridge University Press in 1941.

Much source material comes from government and statutory reports of various kinds, including the Forestry Commission's Annual Reports and its annual Forestry Facts and Figures. These documents are available in specialist reference libraries. The documents have only been noted here where the source is not obvious from the text.

References to the general background history of the economy and the countryside which are unspecific to tree and forest history can readily be found 'on-line' in sources such as Wikipedia.

Introduction

1 Chapman (1941), p. 26.
2 *Sunday Times*, 11 January 2009, p. 8.
3 *News of the World* website, www.newsoftheworld.co.uk/green, accessed 29 October 2009.
4 Anon. (2009), *Common Cause: The Green Standard Manifesto on Climate Change and the Natural Environment*, Green Alliance, London.
5 Lloyd George (1938), p. 754.

1: Beginnings

1 Rackham (2006), pp. 113–16.
2 Coleman (1977), p. 39.

3 White, J. (2007), 'Living History: Does the English Elm have a Future' in *Tree News* (*Sylva*), Spring/Summer 2007, p. 1.

4 Commissioners … into the State and Condition of the Woods, Forests, and Land Revenues of the Crown (1787–93). 'Report' quoted in M. Hadfield (1967), *Landscape with Trees*, Country Life, London, pp. 113–17.

5 Quoted in Hussey's Introduction to D. Stroud (1950), *Capability Brown*, Country Life, London, p. 20.

6 Latham (1957), p. 24.

7 Defoe, D. (1724–26), 'Tour', quoted by S. House and C. Dingwall, 'A Nation of Planters: Introducing the New Trees, 1650–1900' in Smout (ed.) (2003), p. 134.

8 Young, A. (1786), 'A Tour in Wales' in *Ann. Agric.*, 8, quoted in Linnard (2000), p. 134.

9 Johns (1892), pp. 407–9.

10 Inglis-Jones (1971), pp. 169–71.

11 Sang, E. (ed.) (1812), 'Nicol's Planter's Kalendar', quoted in Anderson (1967), Vol. 2, p. 154.

12 Moorwood, W. (1973), *Traveller in a Vanished Landscape: The Life and Times of David Douglas*, Century Books, London, p. 56.

13 Quoted by S. House and C. Dingwall (2003), 'A Nation of Planters: Introducing the New Trees, 1650–1900' in Smout (ed.) (2003), p. 147.

14 Ibid., p. 150.

15 Collins (1978), p. 27.

16 Ernle, Lord (1936), *English Farming Past and Present*, 5th edn, A.D. Hall (ed.), Longmans Green, London, p. 387.

17 Linnard (2000), p. 111.

18 Edlin (1949), p. 88.

19 Brown (1851), pp. 389–90.

20 Royal Commission on Agriculture, 'Reports of Investigators: Buckinghamshire, 13', quoted in P. Horn (1987), *Labouring Life in the Victorian Countryside*, paperback edn, Alan Sutton, Gloucester, p. 106.

21 Forbes (1904), 1906 edn, p. 38.

22 Lorimer, Sir R. (1916), 'The Neglect of Home Timber' in *Country Life*, quoted in the *Transactions* of the Royal Scottish Arboricultural Society, Vol. xxx, p. 104.

23 Rodgers (1941), p. 55.

24 Addison (1977), p. 53.

25 See figures quoted for 1905 in: Forestry Commission (1928), *Report on Census of Woodlands*, HMSO, London, p. 6.

2: Voices for Forestry

1 Anderson (1967), Vol. 2, p. 367.

2 Lothian, Marquis of (1884), 'Address' by the president, reported in the *Transactions* of the Royal Scottish Arboricultural Society, Vol. x, p. 77.

3 Quoted in Richards (2003), pp. xxxv–xxxix.

4 Simpson, J. (1903), *The New Forestry*, 2nd edn, Pawson and Brailsford, Sheffield, p. ii.

5 Royal Commission on Coast Erosion and Afforestation (1909), Second Report (on Afforestation), HMSO, London.

6 Lindley (1935), p. 159.

7 Lovat, Lord and Stirling of Kier, Capt. (1911), *Forest Survey of Glen Mor*, Royal Scottish Arboricultural Society.

8 Lloyd George (1938), p. 751.

9 Milne-Home, J.H. (1915), 'The Home Pitwood Supply', *Transactions*, Royal Scottish Arboricultural Society, Vol. xxiv, p. 1.

10 Postmaster General (1915), 'Supply of Home-grown Telegraph and Telephone Poles', *Transactions*, Royal Scottish Arboricultural Society, Vol. xxiv, pp. 89–90.

11 Forestry Commission (1920), *Annual Report*, No 1, p. 23.

12 Forestry Commission (1924), *Report on Census of Woodlands and Census of Production of Home-Grown Timber*, HMSO, London, p. 14.

13 Pulbrook, E.C. (1922), *English Country Life and Work*, Batsford, London, p. 227.

14 Lindley (1935), pp. 214–16.

15 Ibid.

16 Ibid., p. 62.

17 Quoted in Acland (1981), p. 148.

18 Reconstruction Committee, Forestry Sub-Committee, Final Report (*The Acland Report*) (1918), HMSO, London.

19 James, N.D.G. (1982), *A Forest Centenary: The History of the Royal Forestry Society of England, Wales and Northern Ireland*, Basil Blackwell, Oxford, p. 36.

20 Robson, W.A. (ed.) (1937), *Public Enterprise*, George Allen and Unwin, London, pp. 9–11, 59–72.

21 The Irish connection was relinquished when the Republic of Ireland came into being in December 1922.

22 Lindley (1935), p. 258.

23 McEwen (1977), p. 95.

24 Quoted in Newby (1987), p. 152.

25 Lindley (1935), p. 229.

26 Ibid., p. 255.

27 Jackson, J. (2001), 'Benmore and the Younger Family' in *FCRA* (Forestry Commission Retirement Association) *News*, Issues 14, 15.

28 Lloyd George (1938), p. 753.

29 McEwen (1977), p. 11.

30 McEwen (1998), p. 43.

31 Linnard (2000), p. 160.

32 Forbes (1904), 1906 edn, p. 16.

33 Ryle, G.B. (1972), *Beating about the Bush; Forests, Foresters and the Environment*. Typescript of an unpublished book in the Forestry Commission library, Forest Research, Alice Holt Lodge, Farnham, Surrey, p. 39.

34 Pritchard, H.A. (1928), 'Forest Workers' Holdings', *Journal of the Forestry Commission*, No 7, p. 6.

35 Skipper and Williamson (1997), p. 39.

36 Ryle, G. (1976), 'Forestry' in C. Gill (ed.), *The Countryman's Britain*, David and Charles, Newton Abbott, pp. 116–17.

37 Ibid.

38 Smith, H. and Waygood, G. (2002), The Forester Training Schools. Unpublished papers, 16 September 2002.

39 Linnard (2000), p. 185. Forestry at Bangor is now part of the School of Environment, Natural Resources and Geography.

3: The Ideal Place to Grow Trees

1 Lindley (1935), p. 252.

2 Quoted in Moules, A. (1997), *Talking Taproots*, Quacks Books, York, p. 60.

3 Neustein, S.A. (1976), 'A History of Ploughing' in *Scottish Forestry*, January 1976, p. 6.

4 Wilson, K.W. (1959), 'Crow about Railway Fires', *Journal of the Forestry Commission*, No 28, pp. 190–1.

5 Shaw, D.L. (1971), *Gwdyr Forest in Snowdonia*, Booklet No 18, Forestry Commission, p. 23.

6 Symonds (1936), *Afforestation in the Lake District*, J.M. Dent and Sons, London.

7 Addison, Lord (1939), *A Policy for British Agriculture*, Left Book Club Edition, Victor Gollancz, London, p. 271.

8 Quoted in Sheail, John (1976), *Nature in Trust*, Blackie and Son, Glasgow, p. 84.

9 Hiley, W.E. (1931), *Improvement of Woodlands*, Country Life, London, p. 9.

10 Sheail (1981), pp. 182–5.

11 Quoted in Roberts (1999), p. 160.

12 Quoted in Porter (1994), p. 171.

13 Meiggs (1949), p. 247.

14 Forestry Commission (1943), pp. 1–91.

15 Dalton (1962), p. 59.

16 Ibid., pp. 154–5.

17 The writer remembers this when he worked at Speymouth Forest, Fochabers, Morayshire, in the 1970s.

18 Richards (2003), p. 24.

19 Keenleyside, J., personal communication, 8 May 2005.

20 Stoddart, W.F. (1959), 'Report on Excursion' in *Journal of the Forestry Commission*, No 28, p. 38.

21 Scott, M. (1977), *Reflections, Recollections: A Post War Childhood in Argyllshire*, Janus Publishing Company, London, pp. 82–3.

22 Smith, F.V. (1976), quote from the *Newcastle Evening Chronicle* in May 1964 in *Sociological survey of Border forest villages*, Forestry Commission Research and Development Paper No 112.

23 Ryle (1969), p. 55.

24 Hiley (1964), p. 213.

4: Woods and Private Landowners

1　Brown (1847), 2nd edn, 1851, p. 9.
2　Schlich, W. (1889 onwards), *Schlich's Manual of Forestry*, Bradbury, Agnew, London.
3　Schlich, W. (1904), *Forestry in the United Kingdom*, Bradbury, Agnew, London, p. 70.
4　Copies of these Schlich plans are in the Forestry Commission's library at Alice Holt Lodge, Farnham, Surrey.
5　Forbes (1904), 1906 edn, pp. viii, 30.
6　Since 2003, forestry at Oxford has been part of the Plant Sciences Department.
7　Devonshire, Duchess of (1990), *The Estate: A View from Chatsworth*, Macmillan, London, pp. 69–89.
8　Ward (1952), p. 47.
9　Hopkinson A.D. (1929), 'Afforestation and Unemployment' in *Quarterly Journal of Forestry*, Vol. XXIII, pp. 126–7.
10　The Royal Forestry Society (1930), 'Editorial: Wanted – A Demonstration Forest Estate' in *Quarterly Journal of Forestry*, Vol. XXIV, pp. 1–5.
11　Elmhirst, L.K. (1969), 'Looking Back: Private Forestry', Report of Discussion Meeting 'Forestry Fifty Years On', Reading, 3–5 January 1969, supplement to *Forestry*, Oxford University Press, pp. 22–31.
12　Hiley (1964), p. 23.
13　Ibid., pp. 212–19.
14　Anderson (1967), Vol. 2, p. 502.
15　Hiley (1964), p. 215.
16　Meiggs (1949), p. 39.
17　James (1981), p. 240.
18　Ward (1952), p. 319.
19　Gaze, J. (1988), *Figures in the Landscape – A History of the National Trust*, Barrie and Jenkins with the National Trust, London, pp. 179–80.
20　Centre for Agricultural Strategy (1980), *Strategy for the UK Forest Industry*, CAS Report No 6, Reading, p. 48.
21　Devonshire, Duchess of (1990), *The Estate: A View from Chatsworth*, Macmillan, London, pp. 69–89.
22　Forestry and Home Grown Timber, December 1973/January 1974, p. 4.
23　Bolton (1956), p. 17.
24　Hart (1962), p. 2.
25　Young (1982), p. 288.
26　Marshall, H. (2007), personal communication, 14 September 2007.
27　Writing in Hiley (1964), pp. 217–18.
28　Parker-Jervis, R. (1982), 'The Private Owners' View on Broadleaves' in D.C. Malcolm, J. Evans and P.N. Edwards (eds), *Broadleaves in Britain*, Proceedings of the Loughborough Symposium, July 1982, Institute of Chartered Foresters and the Forestry Commission, Edinburgh, p. 120.

29 Rackham, O. (1976), *Trees and Woodland in the British Landscape*, J.M. Dent, London.

30 Rackham, O. (2001), *Trees and Woodland in the British Landscape*, paperback edn, Phoenix Press, London.

31 Athol, Duke of (1988), Speech at the Scottish Forestry at the Crossroads Conference, 25 November 1988. Quoted in *Scottish Forestry*, 1989, p. 56.

32 Forestry Commission (2003), *National Inventory of Woodland and Trees: report for Great Britain*, p. 28.

5: Afforestation: Land and Landscape

1 Natural Resources (Technical) Committee (1957), *Forestry, Agriculture and Marginal Land*, HMSO, London.

2 Exmoor Society (1959), 'Editorial' in *Exmoor Review*, No 1.

3 Bonham-Carter (1991), p. 32.

4 Miles (1967), p. 117.

5 Ibid., pp. 139–70.

6 Ryle, G.B. (1963), 'National Forests and Parks', *Journal of the Forestry Commission*, No 32, p. 4.

7 Crowe (1956), pp. 43–4.

8 Tompkins (1989), p. 24.

9 Fairbrother (1970), p. 126.

10 Quoted in Sheail (1981), p. 244.

11 Fraser Darling, F. (1974), *The Forest and Global Environment*, address delivered in September 1974 to the Tenth Commonwealth Forestry Conference in Oxford. Forestry Commission, London. (Also reproduced in a shortened form in *Unasylva*, No 27 (1) under the title 'Forestry, the Environment and Man's Needs'.)

12 Crowe (1956), p. 43.

13 Mather, A.S. and Murray, N.C. (1986), *Private Sector Afforestation in Scotland*, Discussion Paper 7, Aberdeen University Geography Department, Aberdeen.

14 Tompkins (1989), p. 52.

15 Boyd (1999), pp. 214–16.

16 Ibid.

17 Ibid.

18 Avery and Leslie (1990), p. 230.

19 Wilkie, N.M. and Mayhew, P.W. (2003), 'The Management and Restoration of Damaged Blanket Bog in the north of Scotland', *Botanical Journal of Scotland* 55(1), pp. 125–33.

20 Royal Forestry Society (1988), President's message in *Quarterly Journal of Forestry*, Vol. LXXXII, No 3, p. 149.

21 Royal Scottish Forestry Society (1988), President's message in *Scottish Forestry*, Vol. 42, p. 91.

22 Crofts, R. (1995), *The Environment – Who Cares*, Scottish Natural Heritage, Edinburgh, p. 15.

23 Bonham-Carter, V. (1972), *The Survival of the English Countryside*, Country Book Club, Newton Abbot, p. 91.

6: The Greening of Forestry

1 Cutter, S., Renwick, H. and Renwick W. (1991), *Exploitation, Conservation, Preservation*, 2nd edn, John Wiley, New York, p. 192.
2 Fairbrother (1970), p. 167.
3 Ibid., p. 327.
4 Grant, W. (1971), 'American Practice in Conservation', proceedings of 11th Discussion Meeting of Foresters of Great Britain, Supplement to *Forestry*, Oxford University Press, pp. 13–23.
5 Hibberd, B.G. (1985), 'Restructuring of Plantations in Kielder Forest District', *Forestry*, No 58, pp. 119–29.
6 Avery and Leslie (1990), p. 100.
7 See, for instance, Bayes, K. (1991), 'Conifer Management and Birds', *Tree News*, The Tree Council, pp. 6–9; and Humphrey, J., Ferris, R. and Quine, C. (2003), *Biodiversity in Britain's Planted Forests*, Forestry Commission, Edinburgh.
8 Avery and Leslie (1990), pp. 183–232.

7: Freedom to Roam?

1 Miller, R. (1981), *State Forestry for the Axe*, Hobart Paper 91, Institute of Economic Affairs.
2 Mason, D. (1991), in Broadcast Reporting Service Tellex Report from BBC Radio Scotland, 4 March 1991.
3 Forestry Commission (1982), 'Guidelines on the Selection of Areas for Disposal', 62nd Annual Report of the Forestry Commission, 1981–82, Appendix V, p. 45.
4 Kirkland, A. and Berg, P. (1997), *A Century of State-Honed Enterprise: A Hundred Years of State Plantation Forestry in New Zealand*, Profile Books, Auckland.
5 Reported in *The Economist*, 15 February 1986, quoted by the Ramblers Association, 1 February 1994.
6 Reported in *The Scotsman*, 9 November 1993.
7 Forestry Commission (1984), 'Disposal of Property Managed by the Forestry Commissioners: A Statement of Policy and Practice', 64th Annual Report, 1983–84, Appendix VI, pp. 50–3.
8 Ramblers Association, Press Release, 22 February 1986.
9 Ramblers Association, Press Release, 1 February 1994.
10 *Country Life* (1994), Editorial, 14 April 1994, p. 39.
11 Forestry Commission, the Scottish Office and the Ministry of Agriculture, Fisheries and Food (1994), *Our Forests: The Way Ahead: Conclusions of the Forestry Review*, August 1994.

12 Buccleuch, Duke of (1993), writing in *Country Life*, November 1993.
13 Hansard (1994), Vol. 247, No 138, Col. 177, 19 July 1994.
14 *The Scotsman* (1994), Editorial, 11 April 1994.
15 Stirling, A. (1994), writing in the National Trust's house magazine No 72, June 1994.
16 Young, B. (1993), writing in the RSPB's house magazine *Birds*, August 1993.
17 Shoard (1995), p. 56.
18 As, for instance, referred to in: Forestry Commission (2006), Annual Report and Accounts, 2005–6, TSO, Edinburgh, p. 74.

8: Timber from the Trees

1 Rose, W. (1943), *The Village Carpenter*, reprinted edn, Cambridge University Press, London, pp. 16–17.
2 Wilson (1980), p. 6.
3 Hart-Davies, A. (2004), *What the Past Did For Us*, BBC Books, London, p. 162–4.
4 Gregory, R. (2005), *The Industrial Windmill in Britain*, Phillimore and Co., Chichester, pp. 103–6.
5 Ibid.
6 Ibid.
7 Sinclair, J. (1791–99), The Statistical Account of Scotland, Edinburgh.
8 Linnard (2000), p. 97.
9 Grant, E. (2006), *Memoirs of a Highland Lady: 1797–1827*, paperback edn, Canongate, Edinburgh, pp. 269–72.
10 'The Monymusk Papers' (1718–55), quoted by I.F. Grant (1961), *Highland Folk Ways*, Routledge and Kegan Paul, London, p. 246.
11 Watson (1998), p. 12.
12 Wilson (1980), p. 7.
13 Watson (1998), p. 8.
14 Wilson (1980), p. 5.
15 Henshaw, H. (1949), *The Use of Timber in Mining*, Timber Development Association, London, p. 8.
16 Venables, C.J. (1969), 'Looking Back: The Home Timber Trade' in Report of Discussion Meeting 'Forestry Fifty Years On', Reading, 3–5 January 1969, Supplement to *Forestry*, Oxford University Press, Oxford, pp. 35–40.
17 Smith, T. (1988), extract from a speech presented at the Home Timber Merchants Association of Scotland Dinner, 16 September 1988 (Author's papers).
18 Wilson (1980), p. 10.
19 Ryle (1969), p. 23.
20 Royal Scottish Arboricultural Journal (1925), *Transactions*, Vol. XXXIX, Part 1, p. 2.
21 Wilson (1980), p. 13.

22 Fitzgerald, R. and Grenier, J. (1992), p. 48.

23 Forestry Commission (1943), p. 23.

24 House, F.H. (1965), *Timber at War*, Ernest Benn, London, p. 2.

25 Goodhart, A. (1997), 'Acquisition' in Anon. (1945), p. 11.

26 Ryle (1969), p. 71.

27 Meiggs (1949), pp. 134–63.

28 Anon. (1945), p. 5.

29 McEwen, J. (1963), 'Wartime Logging Camps in Scotland', *Scottish Forestry*, Vol. 17, pp. 259–62.

30 Extract from a poem (unknown author) reproduced in Grey (1998), p. 184.

31 Stanley, Major G.F.G. (1943), *The Canadian Forestry Corps 1940–1943* (article from an unknown Canadian journal in the library of the Forestry Commission, Alice Holt Lodge, Farnham, Surrey).

32 Wonders (1991), p. 81.

33 Meiggs (1949), pp. 164–89.

34 Asylum Pictures: A Production for Scottish Television (Broadcast 2004), *Treefellers: The story of the Hondurans in Scotland*.

35 *Inverness Courier*, 23 October 1942, quoted in A. Gray (1998), p. 4.

36 McEwen, J. (1963), 'Wartime Logging Camps in Scotland', *Scottish Forestry*, Vol. 17, pp. 259–62.

37 Sutherland, D. (1968), *The Landowners*, Anthony Blond, London, p. 116.

38 Serry, Victor (1967), *British Sawmilling Practice*, Ernest Benn, London, p. 21.

39 Ercolani (1975), pp. 137–40.

40 Edlin, H.L. (1963), 'A Modern Sylva or a Discourse of Forest Trees 4, Oak', *Quarterly Journal of Forestry*, Vol. 57, No 1, p. 23.

41 Anon. (1967), *Journal of the Forestry Commission*, No 35, 1966–67, pp. 120–30.

42 Gamble, B. and Verdon, S. (1989), 'A Forest of Opportunity', *Accountancy*, February 1989, p. 72.

43 'The Eclipse of the Rural World' is Chapter 10 in Newby (1987), pp. 211–37.

44 World Wildlife Fund (2002), *Forests for Life: Working to Protect, Manage and Restore the World's Forests*, WWF, Gland, Switzerland, p. 12.

45 Mathers, M. (1994), 'Timber Labelling', *Reforesting Scotland*, Issue 11, p. 23.

46 Fitzgerald and Grenier (1992), p. 119.

47 United Kingdom Woodland Assurance Scheme (2000), *Certification Standard for the UK Woodland Assurance Scheme*, UKWAS Support Unit, Edinburgh.

9: New Directions

1 Strathclyde, Lord (1991), 'What's New in Scottish Forestry?' Conference, Perth, 26 March 1991, quoted in *Scottish Forestry*, Vol. 42, pp. 221–2.

2 *Reforesting Scotland* (Magazine of Reforesting Scotland) (2007), Issue 16, p. 21.

3 *Reforesting Scotland* (1999), Issue 20, p. 32.

4 *Broadleaf* (Magazine of the Woodland Trust) (2001), Issue 56, pp. 10–11.

5 Hunt, John (2000), 'The Contribution of the Millenium Forest for Scotland

Initiative to Forest Restoration' in the proceedings of a conference on the Restoration of Wooded Landscapes, held at Heriot Watt University, September 2000, Forestry Commission, p. 77.

6   Scottish Forest Alliance website (www.scottishforestalliance.org.uk), accessed 28 August 2009.

7   Forestry Commission (1984), *Broadleaves in Britain: A Consultative Paper*, Preface.

8   House of Lords Committee on Science and Technology, Vol. 1, 'The Sherfield Report' (1980), *Scientific Aspects of Forestry*, HMSO, London, pp. 42–3.

9   As for instance, Peterken, G.F. (1995), 'Foreword: An Overview on Native Woodland Creation' in R. Ferris-Kaan (ed.), *The Ecology of Woodland Creation*, Wiley, Chichester, p. xi.

10 Woodland Trust (2002), *Space for Nature*, Woodland Trust, Grantham; Scottish Natural Heritage and Forestry Commission (2003), *Habitat Networks*.

11 Hunt, John, 'The Contribution of the Millenium Forest for Scotland Initiative to Forest Restoration', pp. 80–1.

12 Ibid.

13 Scottish Forest Alliance website: www.scottishforestalliance.org.uk, accessed on 28 August 2009.

14 As reported in several issues of the Trust's house magazine *Broadleaf*.

15 Harrington-Vail, R. (2007), 'Can Trees Save the Planet', *Tree News, Sylva*, Autumn/Winter 2007, p. 2.

16 Churchill, S. (2006), 'National Forest: the restoration of land and communities' in the papers of the 'New Lives, New Landscapes' conference, 17/18 October 2006, Woodland Trust, Grantham.

17 Webber, J. (2008), 'Greening the Black Country: The Work of the Midland Reafforesting Association in the Early Twentieth Century', *Arboricultural Journal*, Vol. 31, pp. 45–62.

18 Stebbing, E.P. (1919), *Commercial Forestry in Britain; Its Decline and Revival*, John Murray, London, p. 43.

19 Barr, J. (1970), *Derelict Britain*, revised edn, Penguin Books, Harmondsworth, Middlesex, p. 15.

20 Zehetmayr, J. (1979), Introduction to K.F. Broad, *Tree Planting on Man-made Sites in Wales*, Forestry Commission.

21 Fairbrother (1970), pp. 324–8.

22 CJC Consulting, Report to the Countryside Agency (2000), *Economic Benefits of Community Forestry*, Phase 1 Study, Appendix.

23 Woodland Trust (undated), 'Tree for All', p. 7.

24 Starr (2005), pp. 173–80.

25 Forestry Commission (2003), *The National Inventory of Woodland and Trees*, Forestry Commission, Edinburgh, Map 5, p. 48.

26 Figures provided by Bull, Graham, personal communication, Forestry Commission, 22 September 2009.

27 St Barbe Baker, R. (1944), *I Planted Trees*, Lutterworth Press, London, p. 244.

BIBLIOGRAPHY

Acland, A. (1981). *A Devon family: The Story of the Aclands*. Phillimore, Chichester.

Addison, W. (1977). *Portrait of Epping Forest*. Robert Hale, London.

Anderson, M.L. (1950). *Selection of Tree Species*. Oliver and Boyd, London.

———— (1967). *A History of Scottish Forestry*, Vols 1 and 2. Thomas Nelson, London.

Anon. (ed.) (1945). *Meet the Members: A Record of the Timber Corps of the Women's Land Army*. Facsimile edn by Imperial War Museum, 1997.

Avery, M. and Leslie, R. (1990). *Birds and Forestry*. Poyser, London.

Bolton, Lord (1956). *Profitable Forestry*. Faber and Faber, London.

Bonham-Carter, V. (1991). *The Essence of Exmoor*. The Exmoor Press, Dulverton.

Boyd, Morton, J. (1999). *The Song of the Sandpiper*. Colin Baxter Photography, Grantown-on-Spey, Moray.

Brown, J. (1847). *The Forester*. Blackwood, London.

Chapman, D.H. (1941). *The Seasons and the Woodman*. Cambridge University Press, London.

Coleman, D.C. (1977). *The Economy of England 1450–1750*. Paperback edn, Oxford University Press, Oxford.

Collins, E.J.T. (1978). *The economy of upland Britain 1750–1950*. Centre for Agricultural Strategy, Reading.

Crowe, S. (1956). *Tomorrow's Landscape*. The Architectural Press, London.

Dalton, H. (1962). *High Tide and After: Memoirs 1945–1960*. Frederick Muller, London.

Edlin, H.L. (1949). *Woodland Crafts in Britain*. Batsford, London.

———— (1956). *Trees, Woods and Man*. Collins, London.

Ercolani, L.R. (1975). *A Furniture Maker*. Ernest Benn, London.

Evelyn, J. (1706). *Sylva* or *A Discourse on Forest Trees*. (First published 1664 but references in this book from introductory sections of 1706 edn, with preface 'To the King' dated 5 December 1678.)

Fairbrother, N. (1970). *New Lives, New Landscapes*. The Architectural Press, London.

Fitzgerald, R. and Grenier, J. (1992). *Timber: A Centenary History of the Timber Trade Federation 1892–1992*. Batsford, London.

Forbes, A.C. (1904). *English Estate Forestry*. Edward Arnold, London.

Forestry Commission (1943). *Post War Forest Policy*. Report by HM Forestry Commissioners, HMSO, London.

Forestry Commission (2003). *National Inventory of Woodland and Trees: Great Britain*. Forestry Commission, Edinburgh.

Gray, A. (1998). *Timber: Memories of Life in the Scottish Women's Timber Corps*. Tuckwell Press, East Linton.

Harris, E., Harris J. and James, N.D.G. (2003). *Oak: A British History*. Windgather Press, Macclesfield.

Hart, E.C. (1962). *Practical Forestry for the Agent and Surveyor*. The Estates Gazette Ltd, London.

Hiley, W.E. (1931). *Improvement of Woodlands*. Country Life, London.

——— (1964). *A Forestry Venture*. Faber and Faber, London.

Inglis-Jones, E. (1971). *Peacocks in Paradise*. Paperback edn, Service Publications, Shoreham-by-Sea.

James, N.D.G. (1981). *A History of English Forestry*. Blackwell, Oxford.

Johns, C.A. (1892). *The Forest Trees of Britain*. Society for Promoting Christian Knowledge, London.

Latham, B. (1957). *Timber, Its Development and Distribution*. G.G. Harrop, London.

Lindley, F.O. (1935). *Lord Lovat: 1871–1933: A Biography*. Hutchinson and Co., London.

Linnard, W. (2000). *Welsh Woods and Forests: A History*. Gomer, Llandysul.

Lloyd George, D. (1938). *War Memoirs of David Lloyd George*. New edn, Vol. 1, Odhams Press, London.

McEwen, J. (1977). *Who Owns Scotland?* EUSPB, Edinburgh.

——— (1998). *A Life in Forestry*. Perth and Kinross Libraries, Perth.

Meiggs, R. (1949). *Home Timber Production 1939–1945*. Crosby Lockwood, London.

Miles, R. (1967). *Forestry in the English Landscape*. Faber and Faber, London.

Mitchell, A.L. and House, S. (1999). *David Douglas: Explorer and Botanist*. Aurum Press, London.

Moorwood, W. (1973). *Traveller in a Vanished Landscape: The Life and Times of David Douglas*. Century Books, London.

Mutch, W. (1998). *Tall Trees and Small Woods*. Mainstream, Edinburgh.

Newby, H. (1987). *Country Life – A Social History of Rural England*. Weidenfeld and Nicolson, London.

Niall, I. (1972). *The Forester*. Heinemann, London.

Porter, V. (1994). *Tales of Old Woodlanders*. David and Charles, Newton Abbot.

Rackham, O. (2006). *Woodlands*. Paperback edn, Collins, London.

Richards, E.G. (2003). *British Forestry in the Twentieth Century: Policy and Achievements*. Brill, Leiden-Boston, Netherlands.

Roberts, G. (1999). *Woodlands of Kent*. Geerings, Ashford.

Robson, W.A. (1937). *Public Enterprise*. George Allen and Unwin, London.

Rodgers, J. (1941). *The English Woodland*. Batsford, London.

Rose, W. (1943). *The Village Carpenter*. Cambridge University Press, Cambridge.

Ryle, G. (1969). *Forest Service: The First Forty-five Years of the Forestry Commission*. David and Charles, Newton Abbot.

Sheail, J. (1976). *Nature in Trust*. Blackie, London.

———— (1981). *Rural Conservation in Inter-War Britain*. Clarendon Press, Oxford.

———— (1998). *Nature Conservation: The Formative Years*. The Stationery Office, London.

Shoard, M. (1980). *The Theft of the Countryside*. Temple Smith, London.

———— (1987). *This Land is Our Land: The Struggle for Britain's Countryside*. Gaia Books, London.

———— (1999). *A Right to Roam*. Oxford University Press, Oxford.

Skipper, K. and Williamson, T. (1997). *Thetford Forest: Making a Landscape, 1922–1997*. Centre for East Anglian Studies, Norwich.

Smout, T.C. (ed.) (2003). *People and Woods in Scotland: A History*. Edinburgh University Press, Edinburgh.

Starr, C. (2005). *Woodland Management – A Practical Guide*. The Crowood Press, Marlborough.

St Barbe Baker, R. (1944). *I Planted Trees*. Lutterworth Press, London.

Symonds, H.H. (1936). *Afforestation in the Lake District*. J.M. Dent, London.

Taylor, W.L. (1951). *Estate Forestry*. Crosby Lockwood, London.

Tompkins, S. (1989). *Forestry in Crisis: The Battle for the Hills*. Christopher Helm, London.

Ward, J.D.U. (1952). *A Woodman's Diary*. Routledge and Kegan Paul, London.

Watson, N. (1998). *The Roots of BSW Timber plc: 150 Years in the Timber Industry*. St Matthews Press, Leyburn, North Yorks.

Wilson, R.F. (1980). *Adam Wilson and Sons: The History of a Firm of Timber Merchants*. Adam Wilson and Sons, Ayr.

Wonders, W.C. (1991). *The 'Sawdust Fusiliers': The Canadian Forestry Corps in the Scottish Highlands in World War Two*. Canadian Pulp and Paper Association, Montreal.

Young, M. (1982). *The Elmhirsts of Dartington*. Routledge and Kegan Paul, London.

INDEX